MW01283637

ISBN-13: 978-1544818993

TABLE OF CONTENTS

INTRODUCTION

Tell me and I will forget; show me and I may remember; involve me and I will understand—attributed to Confucius (c. 450 BC)

Studies show that as humans, we forget as much as 80 percent of what we read, hear, or learn within a few hours of reading, hearing, and learning it. That's not a few months, few weeks, or even a few days, but a few hours!

What's worse is that we rely on our memory to retain much more than that, and for much longer. We might come up with a great idea, get valuable advice, receive important instructions, or hear a painfully obvious fact and think that it's just too great, valuable, important, or obvious to ever forget. But sure enough, we forget.

Then we do it again.

Not only do we forget the idea or advice, but we forget we even received one in the first place.

The mind is powerful. It has the ability to learn and remember most anything. But just because it can remember anything doesn't mean that it will. More often than not, the mind will forget most information, even if it is useful or important.

To illustrate, in 1885, Herman Ebbinghaus developed and published the concept of the forgetting curve. The curve shows how quickly information is lost if no effort is made to retain it.

Days After Training

Looking at the curve, every hour that goes by, retention drops exponentially. By the end of the day, majority of the information is lost. There are conflicting claims about the exact percentage of the drop, but Ebbinghaus' experiment has been repeated over and over the last 100 years, and the results are always the same. The forgetting curve has stood the test of time.

The reasons for forgetting are many. For one, it's a necessary process. Most of the information we come across day-to-day is useful only for the short term. For example, do you remember which shoe you put on first yesterday? When drinking coffee this morning, do you remember all the places you placed the cup in between sips? Probably not. Such memories are not important so the mind discards them very quickly to free space for information that may be of more immediate value.

Complex reasons exist for what the mind decides to keep and what it decides to throw out. In general, if information is presented in ways that work with the natural rhythm of the brain, the brain is likely to hold on to that information. If information is not presented in such ways, memory of it will be hit or miss. Somethings you will remember well, but most things you won't.

In order to take charge of what the brain keeps, it helps to understand how the mind works and ways it takes in, processes, and stores information. By understanding these mechanics, you'll know the correct ways to present information to the mind, instead of struggling to figure out why nothing sticks.

This guide intends to teach just that by offering creative, yet practical tips and techniques to refine and sharpen your memory. Rather than rely on the happy accident of involuntary memory, you will have full control of what sticks in your mind and have easier access once in there.

Now, there is no shortage of memory books and tools out on the market today. The problem is that most require the use of highly technical systems, so in order to improve memory, you need to learn, understand, and apply a complicated set of instructions. This can be time consuming and demand a lot of effort. Often the system is useful for only a handful of situations, such as remembering names or a grocery list, but fall short in critical areas such as instructions and procedures.

This book takes a different approach by offering tips and techniques that are easy to learn, and more importantly, easy to apply. The suggestions don't require that you waste time learning difficult systems. Instead, they work with the natural way the mind processes information. As a result, you spend less time trying to remember a difficult system and more time remembering the information you need.

Now, if you like challenging systems, they are offered as well. The goal is to provide a comprehensive list of techniques that can be used to remember all types of information. Not every technique works in every situation and not every brain processes information exactly the same, but there are enough suggestions and variations to pick and choose the right method for you and the situation.

The first chapter starts with repetition because it is the easiest and simplest way to remember something. Repetition does not require developing a new skill, learning a complicated process, or applying a difficult routine. You can begin using it right away with a variety of information.

From there the book takes a detour to discuss *factors*–outside of practicable techniques–that enhance and promote better memory. Factors include things like lifestyle, beliefs, diet, and habits. Understanding these factors make repetition and the suggestions in the later chapters that much more effective.

After the discussion on factors, the rest of the book offers an array of memory tips to remember a wide range of information; from facts, data, and lists to procedures, processes, and songs. The instructions are easy to understand and intuitive to follow. If you are ready, let's get started.

Before proceeding, please make sure to download the bonus guide *Triple Your Reading, Memory, and Concentration in 30 Minutes*. It's free and complements this book's advice to guarantee that you learn and remember more, in less time, and with less effort. You can download your free copy at MindLily.com/me.

CHAPTER ONE - REPEAT AFTER ME

Happiness is the longing for repetition—Milan Kundera

Repetition is repeating information that you want to remember. It is presenting a thought, idea, or other material to the mind over and over until it sticks. For example, to remember a new ATM PIN, you would repeat 5689, 5689, 5689 in your thoughts or out loud until it sticks. This is the essence of repetition.

Although basic, repetition is powerful. In fact, it is the most effective way to remember information. Most, if not all, learning involves repetition in one form or another. Many of the memory aids here or in any other program require the use of repetition. For example, if you use the technique of association to remember the list of U.S. Presidents, you still need to repeat the association over and over.

To appreciate why repetition works so well, it helps to understand the two types of memory.

Two Types of Memory

Memory comes in two forms. One form is conscious memory. This type of memory is held in conscious awareness. When you learn or remember something new, you first do so within the "conscious." This means you actively look at the material and attentively make sense of it. Deliberate effort is put forth to hold the thought in the forefront of your mind.

The other form is unconscious memory. Unconscious memory does not require deliberate effort to hold or retain. The information is natural to remember and recall. Often, unconscious memory is self-evident. It is very clear, obvious, and apparent to a person holding it.

It ingrains itself into reality so there is no need to work to remember the information, as it is undeniably obvious.

For example, you know that a square has four sides of equal length. However, at one point, a long time ago, you did not understand this basic concept. You had to learn and memorize the shape, and the process toward memorizing it did not happen with a quick glance. Instead, it took conscious effort.

First, you were given a description, shown a picture, and then presented with a variety of real-world objects that resembled a square. Then, you were tested on your knowledge by picking out a square from an assortment of other shapes or by matching it to images of other squares. As memory of the square had not yet internalized, you had to consciously work at memorizing it.

With *repeated* practice, you began to understand the shape so it began to soak in. Through this repeated exposure, the concept became self-evident, fixing itself in the background of your mind, always there when needed. As an adult, you can now explain what a square is and can easily pick it out in the environment. The memory of it is unconscious. You are not deliberately trying to hold it, though it is at your disposal whenever you need.

These are the two types of memory–conscious and unconscious. The problem with conscious memory is that it is limited. The conscious mind can hold only so much information before thoughts become jumbled and disorganized. What's more, memory in conscious awareness is difficult to use and put to action, often requiring an intermediate step to process before acting on it.

To illustrate, think back to when you learned to drive a car. In the beginning, you had to "consciously" remember and work through all the steps of driving. Each of the individual steps of pressing the gas, steering, braking, and paying attention to traffic signs consumed your awareness.

At this stage, there was no room in the conscious to think about anything else, as all attention was focused on keeping your foot on the pedal, hands on the steering wheel, and eyes on the road. To turn or change lanes, an intermediate step was needed to work out the action of signaling, slowing down, checking the blind spot, and then steering before actually acting. Furthermore, the smallest distractions threw you off balance and caused intense distress.

On the other hand, the unconscious is considerably more infinite. It can hold substantially more information and can organize that information better and for longer. In addition, the unconscious is immensely more proficient at using and recalling that information. With unconscious memory, you don't have to think about the information—you simply act.

After repeating the steps of driving for a few months, the process internalized and became unconscious. You didn't have to think twice about where your feet, hands, or eyes were or what they were doing. Also, turning or changing lanes didn't require taking an intermediary step to work out the details. You simply acted.

In fact, after a few years on the road, the unconscious completely took over the act to the extent that you can probably now drive while talking, texting, fiddling with the radio, lighting a cigarette, and even putting on makeup–all at the same time. This is just one small example highlighting the power of unconscious memory.

Most memory experts and authors define these processes in terms of short-term and long-term, the conscious being short-term memory and the unconscious being long-term. Though these definitions do little to explain what makes memory short-term and long-term. The difference has to do with the capacity and processing power of the conscious and unconscious states.

With that said, any time you want to learn or remember something new, the goal should be to push that information from the limited, inefficient, and temporary conscious state to the more infinite, efficient, and long-term unconscious one. Doing so allows you to access and use the information on the spot, instead of thinking long and hard about it.

The best way to do that is with the use of repetition. As is obvious from the examples of learning shapes and how to drive, the more you repeat or expose yourself to particular information, the more it is internalized. The process is automatic. There is no need to exhort effort, struggle, or force. All you have to do is repeat the information, and the inner workings of the mind take it from there.

This is what makes repetition so effective. By simply repeating a thought or idea, the unconscious soaks it in like a sponge. This is illustrated in Herman Ebbinghaus' other discovery. As shown in the next graph, he found the downward slope of the forgetting curve can be countered simply by repeating the information.

Rate of Forgetting with Study/Repetition

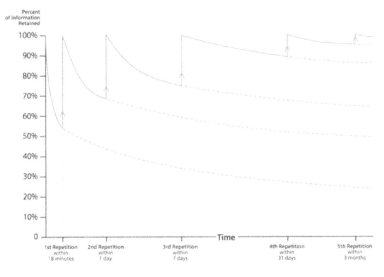

Chi-Ming Ho, 2009

Looking at this curve, forgetting is minimized if there is an attempt to reengage with the information at specific intervals. As the curve shows, if an attempt is made within an hour, memory is back to 100%. After the hour, memory declines again, but not as sharply. Though engaging again within a day, brings it back up. The same applies when reengaging within a week, month, and 3 months.

This principle is the foundation of repetition. Unless information is repeated, it is lost at an exponential rate. To transfer information into long term, unconscious storage, what you do after reading, hearing, and learning is more important than what you do during.

Ways to Repeat Information

Now, when people think of repetition, they usually think of the verbal variety, saying out loud or echoing in their head what they want remembered. Although this is repetition, it is not the only form. Repetition includes reviewing information, like flash cards or notes you've written. It involves listening to something, like a lecture or recording. It also involves taking action on the information.

For example, to remember a lecture, you might start by *taking notes* of the lecture. This is your first repetition. Right after class or at the earliest convenient moment, *review* the notes and edit them to gain additional clarity while the lecture is still fresh. This is the second repetition. Later, *reread* the notes one more time to reinforce the concepts.

After reviewing the notes, attempt to *retrieve* (a technique discussed in Chapter 6) the contents from memory. This acts as yet another repetition. At some point, *test* your knowledge on the notes, which adds an additional round of repetition. If you have time, *rewrite* the notes using different words so that the mind is forced to think about the meaning rather than merely parroting the words. Even *teaching* the information to someone else is a form of repetition.

Revealed just now are seven ways to repeat information and none of them involve verbally echoing the material. If the notes instruct doing something, *acting* on the instructions adds an eight round of non-verbal repetition. The goal is to repeatedly expose the content to the mind in as many ways a possible. The more ways you expose yourself to the info and the more often you do it, the stronger memory of it will become. It's as simple as that.

The key is to repeat the information yourself and not have someone simply repeat it back. If you are given driving directions, for example, hearing the person repeat it won't compare to you repeating it back to that person. If watching an instructional video, re-watching the video won't be as effective as reciting what you saw. Although you could be told something 100 times, it won't connect or register until you repeat it yourself.

Repetition is especially effective for remembering information on the fly. Often the most dire information comes to us when we are not prepared to record it, like the name of a new associate, instructions from a boss, or advice in casual conversation. In such moments, you may not have a pen to write it down or the time to employ a memory technique. You need something that works in that instant, and repetition is great for that.

For example, to remember the name of a person you meet, repeat it a few times immediately after hearing it. Say you meet an acquaintance named Ron. You would say, "Ron, it's nice to meet you, Ron." In your thoughts, repeat the name again, by saying something like "Okay, this is Ron," or "I just met Ron." At the end of the conversation, say the name one last time, "It was good meeting you, Ron." This has given you four opportunities to repeat the name within a few minutes, which increases the chances of locking it down.

In another example, let's say a manager gives you instructions for an assignment. Begin by repeating the instructions back to him or her. "You want me to do this and that, but at the same time, be aware of this other thing?" When your boss confirms, repeat "Alright then, I'll do this and that and keep an eye out for the rest." This presented two opportunities to repeat the instructions.

If a person in conversation says something that you find interesting or useful, repeat the message back with something like, "Just to reiterate," or "Just so I understand correctly," then repeat what they say. Or, if you have a habit of walking into a room and forgetting what you walked in to get, repeat that intention. "I'm going to the closet to get the broom," or "Don't forget to grab the mustard from the fridge."

Finding little ways to repeat instructions, advice, or other messages is extremely effective, and necessary, to remember them. It doesn't take much time or effort and can slip easily into conversation. An added benefit is that the act of repeating forces you to put your own words to a thought while encouraging others to confirm that you got it correctly. This reinforces the content further.

Though repetition is more than raw reiteration. As Ebbinghaus' second discovery shows, there has to be space between the recurrence. Although repeating a name, instruction, or advice in the moment will keep you from losing it that instant, it still needs to be revisited later in that day and next few days to keep the memory strong. It doesn't work to simply repeat a fact 20 times in an hour and expect it to be set permanently.

Remembering Longer Pieces

Sometimes you may need to remember something longer than one word or a small set of words. You may be required to memorize Shakespeare's *Sonnet 116*, Lincoln's *Gettysburg Address*, or the poem "Jabberwocky" from Lewis Carroll's *Through the Looking-Glass*.

Reading a moderately long piece of text several times is not the kind of repetition that usually works. Instead, it is best to learn one small piece at a time and then join those pieces incrementally. It can prove beneficial to have a partner to coach and verify that your memory is accurate.

To do this, take the first line and repeat it. Then take the second line and repeat that. Next, take the first two lines and repeat them together. With this approach of incremental repetition, you build a solid foundation of learning from one end of the piece to the other.

To illustrate, let's take the first sentence of Lincoln's *Gettysburg Address*, a speech given by President Lincoln at the dedication of the Soldiers' National Cemetery during the American Civil War.

"Four score and seven years ago our fathers brought forth on this continent, a new nation, conceived in Liberty, and dedicated to the proposition that all men are created equal."

1. Memorize "Four score and seven years ago our fathers . . . ."

2. Memorize "brought forth on this continent, a new nation . . . ."

3. Memorize (1) and (2) together.

4. Memorize "conceived in Liberty, and dedicated to the proposition . . . ."

5. Memorize (1), (2) and (4).

6. Memorize "that all men are created equal."

7. Combine all parts of the first sentence.

When you have memorized the first sentence and feel comfortable with it, move on to the next sentence. Learn it fully before combining it with the first sentence.

As you will learn in a later chapter, it helps to understand what you are reading, so be prepared to look up words you either don't know or that seem oddly placed. There may be definitions of which you are not yet aware, and without looking them up, the phrase or sentence may seem confusing.

For instance, in the first sentence of the *Gettysburg Address*, the word "score" is not the more familiar sports term, but a word meaning "a group of twenty items." "Four score and seven" refers to "eighty-seven," the number of years that passed from the signing of the Declaration of Independence to when Lincoln delivered this speech.

Using Repetition to Learn a Physical Skill

In addition to remembering a thought or idea, repetition can be used to learn a task, routine, or skill. Memories are stored not just in the mind, but in the muscles as well. When a movement is repeated, over time a memory for it is created in the body, allowing one to perform the movement without conscious effort. The technical term is "muscle memory." So just as the mind needs repetition to memorize information, the body needs it to remember a task.

To commit new responsibilities at work, for instance, in addition to reviewing the instructions, go through the physical motion of the task a few times. If learning to drive a car, go through the steps of braking, putting the car in gear, pressing the pedal, and steering several times before turning the ignition.

Whether you are a white or blue-collar worker, an athlete or artist, a student or caregiver, when presented with a new routine, in addition to reading or listening to the directions, physically run through them several times.

Like memorizing a lengthy speech, it helps to break the task into individual steps and repeat each step on its own before repeating the full routine together. Performing everything at once can overwhelm the mind and can actually make the routine difficult to absorb.

To illustrate, I will share how I learned to salsa. As a person with two left feet and very little experience in any form of dance, getting started with salsa was a challenge. In the beginning, there was too much to take in. In addition to the foot movements, I had to learn to move the hips, count the beat, follow the rhythm of the music, lead my partner, and transition between steps.

Instead of jumping into the full routine, I instead worked on one part at a time. First, I focused on the basic foot movements. I practiced moving the feet and nothing else. I repeated the action of stepping forward with the left foot, rocking back onto the right foot, stepping back with left foot, and so on until the movement became natural and could be done without thinking about it.

Once I had the basic foot movement, I shifted my attention to the hips. Learning to move my hips was tricky as it's an awkward and unusual motion for me. I repeated the hip movement over and over until I got it right. Then I repeated it some more until I was doing it without deliberate thought.

Afterwards, I practiced the foot and hip movements together. I stayed here until the two were in sync.

The next step involved listening to the music and following the rhythm. After gaining solid understanding of the rhythm, I put the three together—moving feet and hips with the rhythm of the music. I repeated the three together over and over until, again, I was doing all three correctly and with little conscious effort.

From here, the next step was added, leading. I studied the proper way to lead a partner and practiced that on its own and then combined it with the other steps. Once all of that was internalized, I was more or less dancing salsa. It was then a matter of incorporating more advanced moves like twirling. Each time I incorporated an additional step, I practiced it separately and then added it to the mix.

Through the simple act of repeating a routine and trusting my mind and body to grasp the movements, I picked up the skill of salsa. More importantly, by breaking the routine into steps and focusing on each step, one at a time, I progressed quickly, more quickly than any other student in the class.

In fact, the other students struggled quite a bit. They couldn't keep all the elements straight in their heads let alone perform them correctly. Many gave up out of frustration or from feeling that they didn't have what it took. Sadly, everyone there had what it took, they just didn't have the correct approach.

With the correct approach, you can learn and memorize just about any physical task, skill, or routine. For example, to learn to shoot a basketball, start first by studying and repeating the proper way to hold the ball. Then study and repeat the proper way to plant your feet. Repeat the two actions together.

Next, learn the correct way to release the ball. Repeat the three steps together. Afterwards, repeat the correct way to jump. Now, you're ready to combine all four, pulling your arms up with the ball, engaging the feet, jumping, and then releasing the ball. To summarize, break the task into individual steps, repeat each step on its own, and then combine them together.

Repetition is critical to learning any skill. Piano players spend hours repeating the right key strokes, basketball players spend hours repeating the ideal free-throw, and baseball players spend their entire life repeating that perfect swing or pitch.

Each one of these skills is learned and remembered through repetition. So, if you want to memorize a task or learn a new skill, repeat it over and over until you have it right. The more you do, the more you will remember.

It is recommended that you limit the number of skills you learn at any given time so that you do not confuse the muscles. For instance, do not attempt to learn how to dance, drive, type, and play the violin all at the same time. You may end up giving a vigorous stroke with your violin's bow only to realize that the bow is the steering wheel of your car in the middle of heavy traffic. Such a vigorous stroke could cause an accident.

It is also recommended that you add short breaks between sets of repetitions to let the rehearsal sink in. Hours of non-stop repetition proves far less effective and sometimes even counterproductive because the body needs time to internalize the movements. Remember Ebbinghaus' second curve, there needs to be space between the repetitions.

Repetition is one method of improving memory, and as observed, it is one of the most effective. Since the technique does not require learning a system or remembering a set of procedures, you can use it immediately and with a wide range of information, especially information that comes at you in the moment.

To truly grasp repetition's astounding power, think about how difficult it is to learn a foreign language. To become a fluent speaker of a dialect, you have to memorize thousands of words of vocabulary, understand numerous rules of grammar, and grasp the many ways to conjugate verbs. In addition, you have to recognize the correct words to use and the proper ways to join those words to make a sensible sentence.

There are so many intricacies that need to be understood and sorted that for many, learning the basics of a new language takes years, and fluency even longer. Although learning a language is complex, each and every one of us has acquired at least one. If you are reading this book, English is likely your native tongue. You are fluent enough to take the words written here and understand their meaning.

Though, consider how you acquired this skill. It was acquired mainly through repetition. From birth, you heard the language spoken in your environment. At infancy, it started with your mom and dad speaking it to you. As a toddler, you experienced it by interacting with friends and relatives.

When slightly older, you experienced additional repetition from reading children's stories, watching TV, and listening to music. Later, you received formal training in the language at school, where repetition helped you learn the correct ways to read, write, and speak. Through persistent exposure, you are now able to speak and understand the complex structure of a language.

What's more interesting is that even individuals who don't go to school or have a formal education pick up the intricacies of a language. Those who grow up in developing nations or in indigenous cultures that lack a formal educational system still develop fluency in their native tongue. They don't have books to read nor do they have classes to attend; they learn simply through the repeated experience of interacting with others in their environment.

This is the amazing power of repetition. With it, you can learn, comprehend, and remember almost anything. So, the next time you get an answer wrong on an exam, miss a vital step in a procedure, fail to master a task, or fall short of understanding a book, don't give up, feel bad, or lose hope. All you need to do is to look at, play with, and review the information some more. If you repeat something long enough, whether it is a dance step or an algebra equation, I guarantee you will learn and remember it.

It is important to note that with repetition, progress is not always consistent or steady. Repeating something twice will not necessarily double your memory and understanding in that very moment. You might repeat something three, four, five, or even six times and sense nothing tangible from your efforts. Then on the seventh try, everything comes together miraculously. Suddenly, the material makes sense and seems intuitive.

Recognize that this inconsistency exists and don't allow it to throw you off base. As you attempt to get a handle on new information, you may feel you are not making any progress or that you're wasting time. Although you are not able to consciously see progress, the unconscious is making headway. Again, don't give up, feel bad, or lose hope. Remain persistent with the repetition and you will achieve the comprehension or memory you seek.

CHAPTER TWO - ATTENTION

Any man who can drive safely while kissing a pretty girl is simply not giving the kiss the attention it deserves—Albert Einstein

Several years ago, a friend was telling me about a nurse that tended to him who had a remarkable memory. She remembered the details of all her patients including the life stories they shared with her. When asked how she remembered such details, she responded "Simple, I pay attention."

As eluded in the intro, the next several chapters cover factors that impact the ability of the mind to retain information. An important factor as it relates to memory is attention. Attention is putting focus on something. It is selectively directing your mind on a subject, object, or thought.

Attention is analogous with awareness, but it is more than that. You can be aware that someone is in the room with you, but your attention might be on a book you are reading. Alternatively, you may be aware of the book, but your attention may be distracted by a pretty face.

One of the primary causes of poor memory is lack of attention. By not paying attention, the mind does not receive information. If the mind does not receive information, it is not possible to remember it. For example, if your boss is discussing an upcoming assignment, yet you are day dreaming about the weekend, you won't "hear" her words. And if you don't actually hear those words, how can they get stored? The brain cannot store what it does not receive.

Furthermore, when you don't pay attention to information, the mind is not able to process it. The mind does not receive enough material from which to make any meaningful sense. Since the mind can't make sense of the information, it is less motivated in trying to record it. For you to make sense of something, attention must take place.

On the surface, all of this is obvious. Of course, you have to pay attention to understand and remember something. As obvious as it though, few truly understand the impact concentration has on their memory and even on their life.

When reading a book or listening to a lecture, we may begin to lose focus, and by losing focus, even for a few seconds or minutes, we miss key information necessary to understand the rest. Since the rest of the content isn't clear, we falsely assume that we are not smart, that we don't have what it takes, or that the subject is just too difficult. And so we give up trying, all because we couldn't hold attention.

Or how about when you go into a room to get something, only to come out empty handed? If a return trip to the room has you coming out empty handed again, you may start thinking you're losing your mind. Again, it's not that you're losing anything, it's just that you're not focused. Most of us are simply not paying enough attention to what we're doing and are either lost in our thoughts or preoccupied with something else.

So, attention is crucial. If you are not concentrating on what you are doing, you are not going to remember it. There is really no way around it. You have to focus on what you want to remember.

Attention comes in two forms—involuntary and voluntary. Involuntary attention arises out of a built-in or inherent interest in something. This type of attention does not require struggle or force as it stems from what feels natural. If you enjoy watching a particular TV show, you will have an easy time paying attention to the story. It will be effortless.

Voluntary attention, on the other hand, requires effort. This type of attention is applied to subjects that are not inherently interesting. It typically involves some struggle or force. If you find calculus boring, you'll likely have to force yourself to stick to the lesson.

To enhance memory, it helps to develop the skill of voluntary attention. Improving voluntary attention nurtures your ability to concentrate on the things you need to remember, especially difficult or tedious subjects like calculus. By concentrating on things in detail, you will be amazed how, often times that is all that was needed to remember information.

Unfortunately, it's easy to say "focus and pay attention," but the reality is, maintaining focus and attention is not easy. It's one of the most difficult skills to develop. In fact, I wrote a book dedicated solely to enhancing this skill, and it's the longest, most challenging book I've written. I've taken some of the concepts and summarized them here to help you acquire and enhance the essential skill of voluntary attention.

Eliminate Distractions

Starting with the obvious, eliminate distractions. In the modern world, distractions are everywhere. Focus declines sharply when the phone is ringing, the T.V. is blaring, or when people are chattering in the background. How well can any single task be performed if attention is split across all these distractions?

Remove as much distractions from your environment. Turn off notifications, close unnecessary apps, shutdown electronic devices, and let calls go to voice mail. If you have a private office, close the door. If not, wear ear plugs. Even consider putting up a sign that says something like, "Hard at Work: Please Come Back Later." The fewer distractions there are, the less your attention is divided among them.

Shift Attention Fully

When you need to shift attention to something important, do so fully. You may be feverishly busy preparing a report at work when the human resource manager stops by to introduce a new employee. If your mind is stuck on the report, the introduction will provide little value. Later, you may not remember the person's name, what he or she looked like, let alone the introduction.

Instead, stop what you are doing and move your attention to the new employee and be critically aware of the temporary priority. To remember such details, redirect attention fully. Don't underestimate the simplicity of this suggestion. You will be amazed at how much memory improves solely by shifting focus fully.

Find Interest

Lack of interest is perhaps the most common cause of poor concentration. When you are interested in something, you typically give that thing a great deal of consideration. While your memory may remain poor on things which do not interest you, you are probably a source of enormous wisdom on topics that do. Everything about that most interesting subject is learned with great ease. In fact, at times it seems entirely effortless, or involuntary, because it arises from a built-in curiosity or desire.

Nineteenth-century French writer Guy de Maupassant once boasted that he could write a story about anything. Someone challenged him to write about an ordinary piece of string. Remarkably, *A Piece of String* became a classic short story even though on the surface it seems to be about an incredibly uninteresting topic.

Renowned American writer Ernest Hemingway once won a bet that he could write a story with only six words—"For sale. Baby shoes. Never worn." Hemingway knew how to sculpt words for maximum interest, and he did not let the constraint of six words stop him from telling a profoundly sad tale.

So how can you turn an uninteresting subject into an interesting one? Start by studying the details. It remains a fact of life that the more you understand something, the more meaning it has. The more meaning something has, the more interesting it becomes.

In Guy de Maupassant's *A Piece of String*, it's the details that make the story so interesting. He describes the moment a man innocently picks up a piece of string from the ground. However, he is accused by a neighbor of having picked up a wallet that had been dropped. In the end, he winds up dying from the shame of having been falsely accused of stealing the wallet. De Maupassant uses a great amount of detail to describe the string, the wallet, and the man picking up the string so that by the end of the story, readers feel great pity for the poor man.

Another option is to connect topics to subjects you do find fascinating. For example, to make art history appealing, you might, as a lover of music, imagine how you would compose a piece of music to portray each artwork. Or, if you are more interested in baseball, imagine each of the artists or the people portrayed in the art playing positions on the field—pitcher, catcher, and shortstop.

If numbers are your fancy, research the current value of each work. Some paintings, once authenticated, are worth millions of dollars. Connecting things in this way can help you develop an interest in art, making it worthwhile to remember.

Practice Voluntary Attention

As you learned in Chapter 1, the more you repeat a skill, the better you internalize it. Well, you can repeat the skill of voluntary attention by noticing the details of articles and objects around you.

To start, pick an item, such as a flower, and notice all its features— shape, texture, color, number of petals, and the way each petal joins to the stem. Touch it. Smell it. If you have a magnifying glass, look at it even more closely. You may be surprised at the number of things you never before noticed.

If you have time, take out a pen or pencil and draw the flower as best as you can. By drawing the item, you will find your powers of observation more acutely focused. Do not worry that your drawing is not of professional quality. The aim is to improve the power of observation, to open the door to interest, and to strengthen attention.

Practice this technique on other things in your environment. Notice the details of cars and buildings in and around the neighborhood. Observe their colors, styles, angles, borders, and how all the parts are connected. When going into the refrigerator, pay attention to everything inside, particularly the packaging and labels of each package. You can do this with people as well. When walking down the street, through the grocery store, or even at the office, examine the clothes, facial features, and eye color of everyone that walks past.

By doing this during spare moments throughout the day, you will build a strong power of voluntary attention—a power essential to building strong memories. In the process, you'll realize that memory is not about having some sort of special gift, but simply about taking the time to willfully pay attention—to what you are reading, what someone is saying, and even to what you are doing.

With practice and the right approach, voluntary attention will turn into an involuntary one. Your mind will start noticing all sorts of details with little effort or struggle on your part. It will happen on its own, making memorization effortless, or at least, easier.

Manage Competing Thoughts

If the previous suggestions don't perk up your concentration, you may have other thoughts competing for your attention. That is, in struggling to finish a sales proposal, you might be preoccupied with thoughts of a party you are attending tonight or the unfinished details of a trip you've planned for next weekend. Since other thoughts are occupying the mind, you are not able to give the sales proposal the attention its due.

When competing thoughts like this become distracting, tell yourself that you will review them at a later time. If several things are crowding your mind for attention, write them all down on a list to review later. Then, set aside time to do just that. You will find that acknowledging the other thoughts by setting a time for when you will attend to them frees the mind to focus on the most immediate mission.

This sums up a key factor in improving memory–concentration. Strong memory comes from strong concentration. In fact, memory is not possible without a certain degree of focus. Therefore, pay attention to the person to whom you are talking, concentrate on the article you are reading, and heed the subject you are studying. Fine tune your voluntary attention so that you can memorize information even if it doesn't necessarily interest you.

CHAPTER THREE - POSITIVELY MEMORABLE

Optimists are right. So are pessimists. It's up to you to choose which you will be—Harvey Mackay

While it is important to pay attention when interacting with new information, to have success in anything, including cultivating a powerful memory, it is vital to foster a strong belief compatible with success. Even if you implement every suggestion in this book, without positive, healthy beliefs, memory can be a constant struggle.

So, what are beliefs?

Beliefs are such a frequently used word that most aren't aware of its true meaning and even less aware of its potential impact on their life. At the most basic level, beliefs are thoughts that you hold or accept to be true. For example, "the sky is blue" is a thought you accept as true.

Inside your mind, you hold all types of beliefs. You have beliefs about your environment, whether it is safe or dangerous. You have beliefs about people, whether you like or dislike them. Above all, you have beliefs about yourself and your abilities. Your "self" beliefs express whether you are smart, talented, and admirable or dumb, inept, and worthless.

Beliefs are powerful–so powerful in fact that they influence a large part of your thoughts, emotions, decisions, actions, behaviors and drives. For example, you may have an unconscious belief that if someone winks at you, they like you. When a person winks at you, you will experience feelings of being liked.

These feelings may consequently motivate you to approach and talk to that person. The response is automatic. You are not thinking or aware of the process; you simply find yourself feeling and acting in accordance with the belief.

Furthermore, beliefs connect to the mind, body, and intellect to mold you into the person you believe yourself to be. If you believe that you are smart, talented, and capable, those beliefs will support you in becoming that person. When faced with a challenge, the beliefs will make the mind sort and operate in ways to see solutions and how to realize those solutions.

If, on the other hand, you don't believe that you are smart, talented, or capable, those beliefs will influence the mind to make you feel defeated, think that there is no solution, or see situations as hopeless. This will lead you to give up without ever trying. If you do try, the negative beliefs will manipulate the mind to overlook key facts, miss vital steps, and make more mistakes than normal to reinforce your presumed inability.

Just as beliefs can influence your emotions and actions, they can in turn influence your physical and mental states. If you have limiting beliefs with respect to memory, such as, "I have a poor memory" or "I can't remember anything," those beliefs will keep you from remembering anything. They will distract your mind when trying to learn, jumble your thoughts when receiving new information, discard information readily, and more importantly, sabotage your efforts to understand and apply the techniques in this book. That's the power beliefs have on our mind and our lives.

It goes without saying then to successfully enhance memory, you must change your internally held beliefs about your ability to remember from "I have a poor memory" to "I have an excellent memory," from "I can't remember anything" to "I have the ability to remember everything." By setting positive beliefs like these, the unconscious will stop sabotaging your efforts to remember and work with you to take in, store, and recall information.

With positive beliefs, memory improvement is intrinsic, meaning you won't have to work hard to store and recall information. It will happen on its own. Much of the resistance and challenge that normally arises when trying to remember will simply disappear.

Affirmations

Unfortunately, beliefs are not easy to change. You can't spontaneously shift your beliefs so that all of a sudden you are able to remember everything. Beliefs take years to form and can take just as long to change. Often, they require the aid of cognitive tools to facilitate the change.

There are many tools to transform beliefs, but none more effective than affirmations. Affirmations are words that you say, write, or think to yourself that reinforce something positive or empowering. "I am confident and self-assured" is an example of an affirmation. Affirming such statements untangle limiting beliefs so you can hone in on and expand your potential—keeping you forward-looking, confident, and strong.

You can use affirmations in this way to hone in on and sharpen memory. With affirmations, you neutralize the negative effects of limiting beliefs and install new, positive ones—those conducive to having a strong and healthy memory.

The great thing about affirmations is they are fairly easy to do. You create positive statements that describe precisely how you want your memory to be and then affirm those statements over and over until the mind is convinced of them.

To help you get started, the following is a list of 10 affirmations that cover common areas of memory one might seek to improve. Repeat each statement out loud or in your mind 8-10 times, each and every day.

1. I have an excellent memory.

2. I remember anything I choose.

3. Every day, in every way, my memory is getting better and better.

4. I easily and effortlessly remember names, faces, places, facts, dates, and events.

5. I recall information quickly.

6. My brain holds information for easy retrieval.

7. My memory provides me with all the information I require.

8. I immediately remember everything that is important to me.

9. Answers come to me when I need them.

10. I have a strong memory of past, present, and future events.

Affirmation Exercise

When affirming the statements, it helps to first slow your thoughts by getting into a relaxed state. When you are relaxed, the unconscious puts up less resistance to the new messages, which allows the messages to more readily harden into beliefs. Here is a soothing exercise to calm down and relax.

Begin by closing your eyes and thinking about a time when you were calm and at peace—perhaps lying on the beach or relaxing up in the mountains. Now take a deep breath, hold it for 5 seconds, and exhale slowly while saying to yourself "relax." Inhale again, hold it for 5 seconds, and exhale slowly while saying "relax." Repeat this 3 more times.

Now that you are at ease, take the previous statements and repeat each 10 times. Affirm the statements with sincerity and certainty, as if they were true, right here and right now. Put positive feelings into the affirmation. After repeating all of them, open your eyes and come back to the present reality. Reciting affirmations this way helps the messages reach deep into the inner conscious to change beliefs at the core level.

Do this exercise twice a day for at least 90 days. The best time to do this is once in the morning, just as you are getting out of bed, and once in the evening, before falling asleep. During these times, the mind is at ease and less resistant to the statements.

In the beginning, it may be difficult to stick with affirmations. As you pronounce a statement, pessimistic feelings in the background may come up, like "this is silly" or "this won't work." The mind may even distract you and make your thoughts drift in another direction simply because it finds the statements too ridiculous. If your beliefs about your ability to remember are really low, affirming the statements may actually trigger physical and or mental pain.

Understand that this is the normal and natural process of changing beliefs. Having a long-standing, strongly held idea in your head makes it extremely difficult to accept a new way of thinking. Thus, the mind will resist the thought since it is not in line with what it already thinks or knows. This is why it helps to get into a relaxed state as doing so eliminates some of the brain's natural opposition to change.

The more you affirm the statements, however, the more the mind will give in to them. The more it gives in, the less resistance the messages will produce. Over time, the statements will transform into new and positive beliefs—beliefs conducive to a strong and healthy memory. At this level, you will easily remember the things you need, often requiring little effort or use of techniques.

Using Affirmations to Improve Memory in Specific Areas

The 10 affirmations listed above focus on core memory issues. The statements were designed to deal with universal memory problems common to most people's experience. However, you may find that there are specific areas in which you struggle more than others.

For instance, you may have a good memory when it comes to remembering chores, tasks, and to-do items, but when it comes to answering questions during an exam, you draw a blank. Perhaps you remember names, dates, and faces just fine, but you have an uncanny ability to forget where you put things. Each person's struggle with memory is unique.

To combat such challenges, you can create statements that target areas that give you the most difficulty. As mentioned, with difficulty during exams, simply create a group of 8 to 12 statements that center on performing well in exams. If you regularly forget where you put things, create a list of statements to better recall where you place items.

To demonstrate, here is a set of affirmations that focus on improving recall during exams.

1. My memory is always clear and sharp.

2. I retrieve answers with ease.

3. As I read each question, answers come to me effortlessly.

4. I trust my memory to provide me with any and all details I am asked to remember.

5. With exams, I remain calm and stress-free. I am not fazed in the least bit.

6. I feel good about myself and my abilities.

7. I let go of distractions and easily concentrate on the test at hand.

8. I am able to recall with vivid clarity everything I study.

9. My mind readily gives me answers I seek.

10. I am a good test taker and always score high marks.

You can create a set of affirmations like this to develop any area that gives you trouble. When it comes to affirmations, you can personalize the statements to you and the area you wish to improve.

Using Affirmations in the Moment

Have you ever been in conversation and drawn a blank on what you were about to say? The information is on the tip of your tongue, but for one reason or another it won't come out. Perhaps you are in the middle of an exam, and you know the answer to a question, but for the life of you, can't call it up in the moment.

In these types of situations, we often get frustrated and ask ourselves questions like, "Why can't I remember this?" Asking a question like this is a destructive affirmation that simply affirms the negative. Essentially, you are telling yourself that you can't remember the thought, and you are looking for reasons as to why. This reinforces your inability to remember.

Instead of affirming a negative statement that is likely to hinder you, affirm something positive. Say to yourself, "I have a good memory. I remember everything I need to recall. The information I need is coming to me." You'll find the information comes more readily this way rather than trying to force the information or figuring out why you are experiencing so much difficulty.

Releasing Negative Thoughts

Perhaps the greatest pitfall in the attempt to affirm the positive is in suppressing negative thoughts. The truth is, negative thoughts are useful. They help us analyze a situation from various angles and arrive at better solutions.

However, a festering negative thought suppressed into the subconscious is like a loose cannon. You don't know when it is going to blow. Suppressing it out of consciousness does not eliminate the problem. It remains far better to shine a light on the negative thought and bring it into conscious awareness by acknowledging the negative and then putting it behind you.

How can you do this? If you feel a nagging worry or have a pestering thought like "I'm going to fail," simply smile to yourself and say, "Yes, I've had problems with memory, but that is changing right now." You can also say, "Well, that's the way it used to be, but things have changed for the better." This faces the negative and defuses it.

Negative thoughts, once acknowledged, can be made powerless. The better you become at recognizing your thoughts and feelings and identifying where they come from, the easier it will be to replace them with empowering ones, allowing you to move forward comfortably.

These are some ways to apply affirmations. The tool has real strength in fostering change, especially as it relates to memory. I have personally witnessed the profound effects affirmations have had on the memories of a wide range of people, whether old and young, rich and poor, men and women.

Having written and taught memory improvement for nearly a decade, I've noticed a common pattern. People who seek to improve memory deep down seek a quick and permanent fix. They don't want to learn techniques, apply systems, or spend a great deal of time and effort remembering information. They simply want their mind to automatically store whatever comes their way.

I suspect that is what you likely seek or were hoping when you purchased this book. If so, this is the only technique that will help you achieve that. Every other technique, whether you learn from this book or another book, requires you to work, engage, and interact with the material. They won't make the information stick simply by reading, hearing, and seeing it.

So, if you take away only one point from this book, it should be the one discussed in this chapter on affirming positive statements. Even if you don't buy into affirmations nor understand how they work, still affirm them daily. Affirmations don't require your approval or understanding for them to work. All they require is that you repeat the statements and repeat them often. By doing so, your memory will improve.

CHAPTER FOUR - OTHER FACTORS

A successful man is one who can lay a firm foundation with the bricks others have thrown at him—David Brinkley, American newscaster

This chapter will cover a few more factors that impact memory before moving to the specific memory techniques. Each of the following principles can be applied to every facet of daily life—school, work, home, and even periods of relaxation. These factors not only aid memory, but understanding them lead to better survival and achievement in the modern world.

Memory and Comprehension

There is a strong correlation between memory and comprehension. The better you understand something, the easier it is to remember. Certainly, one can memorize words from a foreign language without knowing its meaning or memorize a string of letters without knowing the pronunciation, but this is far less effective than memorizing words you actually understand. Memorization through comprehension is more permanent and more useful than memorization by rote.

Therefore, the next time you attempt to commit unfamiliar or complex information, instead of forcing the material into your mind without a second thought, slow down and try first to understand it. Think about the relevance, purpose, or why the content is important. Not only is it easier to memorize information you understand, it usually takes less effort to understand something than trying to remember it, thus saving time in the process.

You Are What You Eat

It should come as no surprise that what you eat affects the brain's performance. The brain gets its nourishment only from the food and fluid you take in, so a well-balanced meal is essential to tip-top mental functioning.

It may sound trite but start each day with a healthy breakfast. Perhaps this advice is given so often because it is true. The brain needs a nutritious spark in the morning to function properly.

In addition to a healthy breakfast, eat plenty of fruits and vegetables. They are ripe with vitamins A, C, and E, beta-carotene, and anti-oxidants. These nutrients help decrease harmful free radicals, which are highly reactive molecules that can damage brain cells. The correct combination of vitamins and minerals neutralizes the negative effects of such free radicals, helping the brain perform better.

In addition, eat more fish. Fish contain the polyunsaturated fatty acid DHA, which contributes significantly to brain development in young children. Kids who eat ample quantities of food with DHA score higher on IQ tests than those with inadequate amounts. Fish also contains omega-3 fatty acids, which are thought to open new communication centers in the brain's neurons. This helps the brain maintain peak performance.

Furthermore, drink plenty of water. Many people take water for granted, but it is one of the most important elements in maintaining brain health, and in turn, healthy memory. The human brain is composed of 70 percent water, so the better hydrated it is, the better it functions. When the brain is dehydrated, it reacts by producing cortisol, a hormone that hinders its capacity to store information.

To ensure you consume a healthy supply of nutrients, it may help to take vitamin supplements. This guarantees the mind receives the vital nutrients it needs. If you take supplements, however, don't use them as meal replacements. As the name implies, they are only supplements, not replacements. Nothing can replace a well-balanced meal.

Memory Supplements

In addition to vitamin supplements, consider taking a memory-specific supplement. Ginkgo Biloba is a popular herbal supplement extracted from the leaf of the Ginkgo tree. With more than 1,000 studies, Ginkgo Biloba is cited as the most documented plant extract used to support brain function.

Studies have found that Ginkgo Biloba improves a variety of brain functions. It has been shown to minimize age-related memory problems (affecting learning, short-term memory, and recall), concentration problems, and absentmindedness. It also helps ease dizziness and vertigo, which often accompany forgetfulness, and tinnitus (ringing in the ears). A 2010 study found that high doses of Ginkgo helped Alzheimer's patients as well.

Ginkgo works in many ways. First, it increases blood circulation to the brain, increasing the supply of oxygen, nutrients, and glucose. This enables neurons to create the energy and other chemical reactions needed to think and remember. It also boosts circulation to the inner ear, thus explaining its power to heal tinnitus and dizziness, a malfunction of the nerves in the ear. In addition, Ginkgo protects against free-radical damage and reduces inflammation. This further improves circulation by keeping the cardiovascular system in shape and also protects the nerve cells themselves.

To use this supplement, it is recommended that you take an extract standardized to 24 percent flavone glycosides and 6 percent terpene lactones or take capsules of the dried herb. For prevention, take 40 mg of standardized extract or 120 mg of capsules daily in divided doses. A person exhibiting mild-to-moderate symptoms may take up to three times this dose. Some people notice an improvement within two to three weeks of beginning treatment, but in most cases, Ginkgo requires at least three months to see full benefits.

You may be asking, what are the side effects of this herb? Gingko Biloba is essentially devoid of any serious side effects. Some people report mild headaches for a day or two when starting the herb, while others have reported mild stomach upset.

Nonetheless, be cautions when taking Ginkgo. Do not use it if taking blood-thinning medication, including aspirin or ibuprofen, because Ginkgo can add to the thinning effect. For this reason, avoid taking Ginkgo for two weeks prior to any surgery, including oral surgery.

Now that you have an idea of what you should be doing as it relates to supplementing your diet, let's discuss things to avoid. As much as possible, avoid fatty foods. They are not only bad for the body, but also for the mind. Replace such foods with the previously mentioned vitamins and minerals.

In addition, quit smoking. Smoking has an adverse effect on the brain's ability to manage information. Visual and verbal memories are especially hard hit with smoking. If you are a smoker, consider not only the health hazards, but the sacrifice of memory, too.

Naturally, if you feel that your memory is not what it used to be, consult a physician. Memory loss can sometimes reveal a far more serious problem—perhaps a disease—that can go undetected for years unless a person takes action.

So, remember to eat healthy. Your mind and memory will thank you for it.

Curb Stress

Another lifestyle factor that zaps memory is stress. Stress is a feeling of pressure or lack of control. It is an emotional response to circumstances, conditions, or events—like bills to pay, boss to please, or colicky baby to pacify. Positive or negative life changes from the joy of a wedding to the loss of a loved one are also stressful circumstances. Stress can also be caused by inner conflict.

Feeling stressed is, of course, just another part of being human. However, overwhelming stress can take a tremendous toll on one's overall health, not to mention memory.

Stress impacts memory both physically and mentally. Physically, stress elicits the release of chemicals that impair proper functioning of memory. Mentally, stress overwhelms and overburdens the mind so that it is unable to think about, focus on, or process information properly.

Dealing with stress is a huge task. It is impossible to eliminate stress with just a snap of a finger; however, there are things you can do to manage it better. The following tips provide some effective strategies to lower stress, and in turn, boost memory and retention.

Avoid Pressure—Putting pressure on yourself to work hard is not a bad thing, but pushing yourself too hard can be. In the long run, it proves counterproductive. This is especially true when cramming loads of facts and data when studying as it puts excessive stress and strain on the mind. This strain impedes both learning and memory. With that said, avoid pressure and loosen up. Doing so leads to better comprehension, and hence, better memory.

Schedule Down Time—Everyone needs breaks from work and study. Instead of using lunch or coffee breaks to catch up on unfinished tasks, spend down time doing something completely unrelated to work. Time off is absolutely essential in recharging the body and mind.

Avoid Non-Pertinent Issues—Don't bring up past grievances or troubles you've had with a subject, even if they deal directly with the present discussion. If you know that certain subjects cause bitterness and resentment, don't bring them up deliberately or in negative ways. Focus simply on the task you are trying to remember. Pay attention to one thing at a time. Sticking to the topic prevents other issues from complicating the picture, thus easing the load on memory.

Learn to Say No—Never feel obligated to take on extra assignments or to do special projects that aren't required but only bring feelings of anger and hostility. Saying "yes" all the time makes us feel helpless, while being able to say "no" gives us a feeling of control and satisfaction. This isn't the same as not wanting to be involved and committed. Allowing yourself the choice of what to commit to and be involved in is the kind of control that reduces stress.

The items discussed here and in the previous two chapters are the main factors impacting memory. Although they are not techniques that directly aid recall, they have a profound influence on memory. Understanding and recognizing these factors make the difference between having a good memory and having an excellent memory.

CHAPTER FIVE - ASSOCIATING WITH THE RIGHT CROWD

A man only learns in two ways, one by reading, and the other by association with smarter people—Will Rogers

With the discussion on important factors out of the way, we can now turn attention to specific memory techniques. One useful technique uses associations. An association is connecting a topic you want to remember with something you already know or with something that may prove easier to learn.

Associations are effective because everything you know, every idea you have, and every thought in your head is linked to or "associated" with other thoughts and ideas. Chad Helmstetter explains this concept in his book *What to Say When You Talk to Yourself*:

> Every new thought you think has to have some old thoughts to stick to, a proper place to fit. When you are told something new, your brain will, in a fraction of a second, scan through literally millions of mental filing cabinets, filled with every idea or thought or impression you have ever stored. In that same fraction of a second, based on the information already stored in your mental files, your brain will send you an instant telegram, telling you how to feel about this new thought, where it should get filed, and whether you should accept it, believe it, keep it, and use it, or disapprove, disbelieve, and throw it out.

As you can see, your thoughts are not stored individually. Rather, they are linked together like an intricate web.

To further illustrate, have you noticed how older generations always reminisce about the past? They say things like, "When I was young, ice cream used to cost…," or, "When I was your age, we didn't have…." Now with the evolution of the e-reader, they will be uttering, "Back in my day, there were no such things as e-books; we read books on paper and carried them in a book bag. And they were heavy."

They speak this way because of the power of association. As mentioned, each memory we have is connected to other memories. When we have a thought, it activates memories associated with that thought, which triggers related memories and experiences.

If you ask your grandma to go for ice cream, for instance, the phrase "ice cream" might trigger a childhood memory of when she had really good ice cream. This will elicit a memory of the price she paid for that ice cream, which is why she might say, "When I was your age, ice cream used to cost…." That memory may trigger other memories about the time, so she will add, "When I was your age, we didn't have…."

This is the reason older generations always reminisce about the past—because all of our thoughts are connected to each other. As annoying or comical as this is to younger generations, when they grow older, they too will talk this way. There is no avoiding it. It is simply the way the mind works. It stores and recalls information based on associations made with other thoughts.

Since the mind works by making associations, you can use this property to improve learning and memory by connecting facts you want to remember to other information. By actively finding ways to create links with other data, you build connections that the mind would not otherwise have or would have to figure out on its own.

The greater the number of connections you build for your mind, the easier a topic will be to remember and recall. More importantly, the associations you create will serve as cues to trigger the retrieval of the newly stored data.

Two commonly used association techniques are acronyms and acrostics.

Acronyms

An acronym is an invented word or phrase made up of the first letters of the items you want to remember. RAM is an acronym which stands for "**R**andom **A**ccess **M**emory"—a computer term. NASA is another familiar acronym that stands for "**N**ational **A**eronautics and **S**pace **A**dministration." This government organization has created numerous acronyms, including LEM (**L**unar **E**xcursion **M**odule) and many others related to spacecraft and space missions.

Sometimes an acronym is far more familiar than the words it represents like SCUBA. The acronym stands for "**S**elf-**C**ontained **U**nderwater **B**reathing **A**pparatus," but in modern English, we simply say "scuba."

Acronyms allow a person to associate a long sequence of items with a smaller word or set of words that you already know. The shorter word or phrase is easier to remember and acts as a cue to help recall the longer piece.

Creating acronyms is straightforward. Start by taking the first letter of each word in a list. Then, rearrange the letters to form a new word or expression that is simple to remember. To remember the color sequence in a rainbow—Red, Orange, Yellow, Green, Blue, Indigo, and Violet—you could take the first letters of each word and create the fictional name ROY G. BIV.

Or let's say you are studying the water cycle in nature and want to memorize the more prominent parts of the cycle—evaporation, condensation, precipitation, runoff, ocean. Taking the first letters of each word gives E-C-P-R-O. From here, you can rearrange the letters to form the words ROPE-C, COPE-R, or COPER.

Acronyms can also include non-initial letters as in radar (**ra**dio **d**etection **a**nd **r**anging), sonar (**so**und **n**avigation **a**nd **r**anging) or amphetamine (**a**lpha-**m**ethyl-**ph**enethyl**amine)**.

You can organize the letters to form a word you already know or make up a word. Often you are limited by the letters with which you are working, so it might be necessary to make up a word or phrase. Making up words or phrases aid the process as it gives the information a personal touch.

Acrostics

A problem with acronyms is that to create a meaningful word, you have to rearrange the letters, which makes it difficult to remember items in sequence. A more versatile tool for remembering a sequence of items is the acrostic.

An acrostic is a sentence where the first letter of each word serves as a clue to an item you want to recall. "**M**y **V**ery **E**ducated **M**other **J**ust **S**erved **U**s **N**ine **P**izzas, was used in astronomy to relate the sequence of planets in the Solar System. It stood for "**M**ercury, **V**enus, **E**arth, **M**ars, **J**upiter, **S**aturn, **U**ranus, **N**eptune and **P**luto."

I say "was" because Pluto has since then been demoted to a dwarf planet. An updated acrostic might be, "**M**y **V**ery **E**ducated **M**other **J**ust **S**erved **U**s **N**uts." The image of a mother serving you and your friends nuts proves far easier to remember than the force-fed memorization of the name of each individual planet.

Another acrostic found in astronomy involves the sequence of star types from hot and bright blue-violet stars (O-type) to cool and dim red dwarfs (M-type). The acrostic famous to astronomy students for over a century is "**O**h, **B**e **A** **F**ine **G**irl/**G**uy; **K**iss **M**e" for the sequence, "O, B, A, F, G, K and M."

To create your own acrostic, start the same way as with an acronym, by taking the first letter of each word in a sequence. However, instead of rearranging the letters to create a new word, come up with words for each letter that together form a clever sentence. Using the water cycle example (evaporation, condensation, precipitation, runoff, ocean), you could create the following sentence "**E**very **C**ook **P**eels **R**ed **O**nions."

Often it helps to make the sentences quirky and funny. Whatever is ridiculous or funny catches the attention of the mind. Plain and boring, by nature, does nothing to catch the mind's attention. A variation on the previous model can be "**E**very **C**lown **P**eels **R**ed **O**nions." The mental image of this is pretty ridiculous, but memorable.

Acrostics can be a great way to remember passwords since most passwords come in a string of letters and numbers. All you need to do is take those letters and come up with a word for each one that combine to form a memorable sentence. The sentence then not only helps you remember each letter of the password, but the exact order as well.

A simple way to do this is to pick a sentence from your favorite book and take the first or last letter of each word in the sentence to form your string or series of letters. Let's use the first sentence of the previous paragraph as an example. Taking the first letter of that sentence "<u>A</u>crostics <u>c</u>an <u>b</u>e <u>a</u> <u>g</u>reat <u>w</u>ay <u>t</u>o <u>r</u>emember <u>p</u>asswords," we get the following series of letters acbagwtrp. Voila–you now have a unique yet memorable password.

If a password requires numbers, then count the letters in the sentence and add that to the end. Our sample sentence, "Acrostics can be a great way to remember passwords," has 42 letters, so the password becomes acbagwtrp42. Instead of having to remember this complex series of letters and numbers, simply remember the sentence, which is far easier.

These are some basic and rather traditional association techniques that you likely already know or have experience using. They are presented to prime the pump for the more sophisticated and advanced methods that follow.

Facts Association

Acronyms and acrostics are great for remembering a list or series of items, but what if you wish to remember something different like a fact, statistic, or other type of data? You can't really take the first letter of a fact and create a new word or sentence. Such information requires a different approach.

Luckily, association can be applied many ways. In fact, the possibilities are endless. Some popular ways include connecting the fact to information you already know, digging into the details of the fact, comparing and contrasting it to similar information, or putting the fact through a rigorous examination. The rest of this chapter examines these options.

Connect to Information You Already Know

One effective way to create associations is to connect facts you want to remember to information you already know. What you already know is the key to learning new information because such information is already fixed in the brain. Since it already resides there, you don't have to spend time and effort planting it. Information that is already planted is easier to recall, making easier to recall any other material you attach to or associate with it.

For example, when presented with the fact that a tomato is really a fruit, think about the characteristics you know about "fruits" such as apples, then compare those characteristics with a tomato. Both are red. Both have seeds. Both are delicious in salads. And so forth.

Keep in mind that with this method, the point is not to learn additional details. You simply want to use what you already know, even if it doesn't relate directly to the new information. The goal is to connect it to memories that are already planted. These memories then provide the roots to support the new data.

How about committing the original thirteen U.S. colonies that declared independence from England to form the United States— New York, Pennsylvania, New Jersey, New Hampshire, Massachusetts, Connecticut, Rhode Island, Delaware, Maryland, Virginia, North Carolina, South Carolina, and Georgia?

As a sports fan, you can connect each state to a major league team home to the state—New York to the Yankees, Pennsylvania to the Phillies, New Jersey to the Nets, and so on. If you know more about athletes themselves, try associating a favorite athlete to the state they are from—Kobe Bryant from Pennsylvania, Dennis Rodman from New Jersey, and Michael Jordan from North Carolina.

You don't like or know anything about sports you say? How about movies? Pick movies that take place in these states, like *King Kong*, which took place in New York, *The Sixth Sense* in Pennsylvania, and *Friday the Thirteenth* in New Jersey.

Are you a bird lover? Associate each state to the state bird. Or if you like music, you can connect the home state of your favorite singer or song writer. Then to call up the list, simply think of the teams, players, movies, birds, or singers.

This strategy can be applied to countries, like those involved in World War I. Since most of these countries are European, a sports fan might associate them with famous European soccer clubs, connecting Manchester United to England, AC Milan to Italy, and Bayern Munich to Germany.

Even a food connoisseur can use this trick by associating cuisine or dishes unique to each country: baguettes and fondue to France, bratwurst and sauerbraten to Germany, pasta and risotto to Italy, and kebabs and boar-ek to Turkey. Using soccer clubs or food may be the perfect hint you need to summon the countries involved in WWI.

These are some ways to associate facts to information you already know. This list in no way all-inclusive. It's a matter of experimenting and practicing. In your experimenting efforts, recognize that each person's mind correlates information a bit differently, so what may seem odd to one person may be the glue for you.

Details

A quick way to create associations is to study the details of a fact. To note that the Nile is the longest river in the world, you might learn other facts about the Nile like where the river is located, the countries it flows through, and more importantly, its length. You might also learn about the wildlife unique to the region or even the major dam built on the river.

Learning such details about the Nile injects numerous associations so it is no longer an isolated thought floating aimlessly in your head. Instead, it is joined to other thoughts and data, securing it for easy memory and recall. By thinking of Africa, the continent where the river resides, or Egypt, the country through which it flows, you can easily stimulate memory of the river.

Revisiting the previous example of the major countries involved in World War I, instead of trying to shove the countries as a boring list, you might learn about the leaders of those countries, the major alliances in the war, the politics behind the conflict, or even how the conflict started. You might also look at the outcome of the war, including the nations that came out winners and those that suffered defeat.

Again, understanding these details sew links and hooks in the mind. These links and hooks then become cues to help recall the countries that fought in WWI. Recalling one nation like Germany may elicit recollection of the Central Power alliance to which it belonged. Thinking about the Central Power may help trigger memory of other countries in the alliance like Bulgaria and Austria-Hungary.

Thinking about Austria-Hungary may then remind you of its tense relationship with Serbia and how the Serbian assassination of Austria-Hungarian Archduke Franz J. Ferdinand was the spark that ignited the war. Through these details, you are able to trigger a host of countries involved in the Great War.

Compare and Contrast

Another way to create associations is to draw parallels or distinctions to similar information. Let's return to the Nile again. Consider comparing it to other notable rivers like the Amazon in South America, the Mississippi in North America, the Danube in Europe, or the Mekong in Asia.

In comparison to the Amazon, the Nile is the longest river in the world, whereas the Amazon is the largest. The Nile is in the northern hemisphere, so it flows away from the equator into the Mediterranean Sea, while the Amazon, in the southern hemisphere, flows towards the equator into the Atlantic Ocean. The indigenous communities around the Amazon exist in small tribes that hunt and fish for food. The indigenous around the Nile River may have begun that way, but they went on to build one of the greatest civilizations the world has known.

It's clear to see that drawing parallels or distinctions in this way lends its way toward building associations that would not normally exist. It's these associations that secure information in the mind. In this example, you secured facts about the Nile River to ideas like the Amazon River, Mediterranean Sea, Atlantic Ocean, indigenous culture, and Egyptian civilization. Calling to mind any one of these items can be instrumental in recalling pertinent facts about the Nile.

Examine

A direct approach to associating facts, data, or statistics is with a thorough examination. With examination, you ask yourself a set of questions that forces you to dissect a particular fact or data. It is kind of like studying the details, but the process is a bit more structured.

To examine a fact, data, or statistic, ask yourself the following set of questions.

1. Where did the information originate?

2. What are my thoughts about it? How do I feel about it?

3. What are its attributes, qualities, and characteristics?

4. What is it good for?

5. How may it be used?

6. How will this benefit me?

7. In general terms, what do I already know? What have I heard and from whom and when?

8. What things can I most readily associate with it? What is it like?

9. What does it prove? What can be deduced from it?

10. What caused it?

11. What history holds it?

12. What are its natural results? What happens because of it?

13. What is its future and its natural or probable end or finish?

Putting facts through such an examination gets the mind thinking about how those facts relate to other information. As you know, the more aware the mind becomes of existing relationships, the more associations it can form, which equates to more ways information can latch onto the brain, which in turn provides more cues at your disposal to retrieve the information.

So how would something like this work? Let's put the Battle of Bull Run, the first major land battle of the American Civil War, through the filter of the preceding thirteen questions.

1. Where did the information originate? The Battle of Bull Run is printed in the American history textbook. Every time you remember American history, this fact will be associated with it.

2. What are my thoughts about it? What are my feelings with regards to it? Your thoughts might be, "Wow, this is cool!" or "Egad, this is cruel and immoral!" or, "It was a necessity to keep the nation together."

3. What are its attributes, qualities, and characteristics? The qualities or characteristics are that it was the bloodiest battle in American history up to that point.

4. What is it good for? It is good for understanding the events that led to the Civil War.

5. How may it be used? It can help you understand why the war escalated to such an extreme level and the strategy the Confederacy used to win the battle even though they were the underdogs. The fact that it was the bloodiest battle in American history up to that point could serve also as a reminder about the violent consequences of war.

6. How will this benefit me? In your day-to-day life, remembering the facts of the battle may not have much value. However, knowing the information may prove useful on an exam.

7. In general terms, what do I know about it? What have I heard and from whom and when? You may know that the Battle of Bull Run was the first major land battle of the Civil War. You may also know it as First Manassas, the name used by the Confederates.

8. What things can I most readily associate with it? What is it like? You can liken the battle to be a stepping stone in abolishing slavery in the United States. You can also make a connection to Abraham Lincoln, since he served as president during the battle.

9. What does it prove? What can be deduced from it? It proves how damaging war can be. It also proves how a mere battle can escalate into a full-blown war.

10. What caused it? Many things led to the battle of Bull Run. It started with Abraham Lincoln winning the presidential election of 1860. Southerners were threatened by Lincoln's policies and felt separation was their only option. This caused states in the south to secede from the U.S. to form the Confederate States of America. On April 12, 1861, the Civil War began as confederate forces attacked U.S. forces at Fort Sumter. This led to the Battle of Bull Run.

11. What history holds it? This one is obvious. It is part of American history, specifically the Civil War.

12. What are its natural results? What happens because of it? A lot happened as a consequence of Bull Run. It set a precedent that the Civil War would be longer and more brutal than anyone predicted. Prior to the battle, everyone expected a short war. In fact, the battle was initially viewed as a spectator event with civilians sitting on hillsides with picnic baskets, watching troops fight as if it were a form of spectator event. After the battle, however, people quickly became aware of its severity.

13. What is its future and natural or probable end or finish? Its future is that the battle ended with an unexpected victory for the

Confederacy. Had the Union won, the war would have been over. Since they lost, it turned into a confrontation that lasted nearly four years.

This is how to build associations via examination. Creating associations this way forms loads of connections. After reading this example, even if you never again hear about the Battle of Bull Run, you will probably remember for a long time that it was the first major battle of the American Civil War.

This is the essence of associations. You take information that you wish to record, then seek ways to connect it to other information you already know or find easier to remember. It's a great way to record vital information.

CHAPTER SIX - RETRIEVAL

It's great to reminisce about good memories of my past—George
Foreman

One of the most powerful learning and memory strategies you are
probably not using, or may have never heard of, is retrieval.
Retrieval is the simple act of recalling information from memory. It
involves spending a few minutes deliberately calling to mind
material you have read, heard, or watched instead of re-reading, re-
hearing, or re-watching it.

After reading a chapter in a book, for example, close the book, and
attempt to recall as much of the chapter without looking at either the
chapter or your notes. Or after a meeting ends, think about
everything that came up in the discussion. You can think of retrieval
as a mental review.

Countless studies show that retrieval is one of the best ways to
reinforce memory. One study, by Jeffrey D. Karpicke at Purdue
University, showed that retrieval not only reinforces memory better
than other methods, but even better than combinations of other
methods.

Retrieval works so well because the real challenge of learning and
remembering is not with putting information in your head—that is
actually natural and easy for the brain to do. The real challenge lies
in getting the information out.

To better explain, if I ask you to recite lyrics to your favorite song,
you may find it difficult to do. I bet, though, that once the song starts
playing, you'd be able to sing along without any problem.

Or you may think you have forgotten much of your childhood memories, but as soon as you see a photo from childhood, everything surges back like you were there yesterday.

In another scenario, have you ever forgotten what someone has said, but the moment they start repeating themselves, it all comes back? They don't have to finish repeating themselves before you're saying, "Oh yeah, I remember that."

These examples illustrate that memories can be stored in the brain yet seem like they are forgotten. The memories are there, but for one reason or another, you can't get them out in the moment you need or want them out.

The reason you can't get them out is because you don't have a clear path or an easy way to access the memories. It's like filing documents in a drawer and forgetting which drawer you put them in. The documents are there, but you don't know in which drawer to look.

With retrieval, you create "pathways" that lead to the memory. Literally, in the mind, a neural pathway is created. It's akin to leaving a trail of footprints or breadcrumbs. Each time you attempt to recall a piece of information, those footprints become deeper. So, in the mind, the neural pathways actually deepen.

This helps the brain clearly see the route to a specific memory. Without a clear path, the mind is lost in the woods, unable to find where the memory is stored or how to get to it. The more you practice recall, the deeper the path gets, and the easier and quicker it is for the brain to "retrieve" that piece of information from the filing cabinet of your mind.

So anytime you read, hear, watch, learn, or do something that you want to conserve, spend a few minutes throughout the day recalling it. Start your first recall right after the reading, hearing, watching, learning, or doing. Since we lose as much as 80 percent of what we come across within a few hours, you want to recall as much of that as quick as possible. Then, practice a few more times throughout the day, and finally, once more before going to bed.

To demonstrate, after getting out of class, while walking home or to the next class, think about what you just learned and the key ideas the teacher taught. Or, as you head back to your desk from an important meeting, review in mind the main points that were discussed and the key tasks you now have to tackle. After hanging up the phone, quickly review the conversation and the notable takeaways.

Later in the day, call up these things again. "I had a conversation with mom, she wanted me to pick up her mail." "It was an interesting article I read on the commute to work…the article said, this, this, and that." "These are the points that came out of this morning's coaching session." "The key takeaways from the podcast were…." And then of course, repeat this in the evening and one last time before going to bed.

Depending on the importance and length of time you seek to retain that info, carry the exercise into the next few days. You don't have to perform it as frequently in the subsequent days; once or twice per day is enough. After a few days, you'll have a solid foundation for that memory and will be able to recall it more readily–as opposed to the alternative, which is that you will likely forget it completely.

To ensure the material locks in for the months ahead, a weekly review is suggested. At the end of the week, recall everything that you have done, learned, and come across. This will really fix the content in the long-term, unconscious storage so you can have instant access without taking an intermediary step to think about it.

The previous suggestions work well for day-to-day encounters, so let's now turn our attention to how one might apply retrieval when studying. Say you just spent a few hours reading, taking notes, and reviewing several chapters of a book. Now close the book, put away the notes, and without looking at any other material, elicit everything that you read, learned, or attempted to memorize.

Remember, don't look back at the material or notes. The entire process must come from your mind. Using notes or other aids is not applying retrieval. It is simply reviewing.

If you get stuck at a specific idea or concept, sit for a moment until the memory appears. Don't give up thinking its lost. When a memory doesn't surface the instant we want it to, it is easy to assume it is forgotten. You likely didn't forget, you just need to give the brain a few moments to shuffle through the mental forest. The key is to not force the memory, but instead to relax and let it come.

If you stay stuck for an extended period or don't know where to begin, try to recall anything. Then use the power of association to steer toward the precise information you seek. When drawing a blank in an attempt to recall the earlier chapters of a book, start with the middle or later chapters or with any part that comes to you easily.

You might be thinking about an interaction between several key characters in chapter 7, and then realize one of them was introduced in chapter 3. Then from there, other parts of chapter 3 appear. You can use this to guide recollection of chapters 1, 2, or even 4. Work through the details of what surfaces easily and use that to recall other items related or associated to it.

When you're confident that you've recalled everything, revisit the passage or any notes you took to verify that what you remembered was accurate and complete. It can help to underline important areas while reading, then go back to review those areas. Adding this process of review after recall ensures that you remember everything correctly and that the memory remains fresh.

Another tip is to spend a few minutes recalling what you already learned before moving further. If you have been studying for a few hours, take a break and recall what you learned so far before stepping into the new information. This ensures the new content doesn't push out and replace the earlier material you spent time acquiring.

You can even do this before a lecture or presentation. As you wait for a class to begin, think briefly about the content that was covered in the previous class, the class before that, or any other material or assignment that led up to the current class. This adds another round of retrieval to the information, but more importantly, it prepares you for the new content that is about to come.

Now, in the beginning, retrieval may not be the easiest technique to apply. In fact, it might prove downright agonizing. Getting lost in random thoughts is often times more enjoyable than forcing yourself to remember information that may not be as fun or exciting. However, retrieval gets easier after a few rounds of practice, and with consistency, it becomes almost automatic.

A major benefit of retrieval is that it immediately identifies gaps in your knowledge or understanding. When you are not able to retrieve information you've read or heard, you immediately know that you haven't fully understood or memorized the material. This signals that it may be an area you need to dedicate more time and effort.

This level of feedback is not possible with any other technique. Instead, one is left with a false sense that they know the topic, lesson, or discussion better than they truly do, especially if the information was easily learned or feels fluent. Don't let such feelings convince you that the content is fresh. Put it to the test by attempting to recall it without the aid of any other material.

What's more, regularly practicing retrieval makes the brain automatically start remembering more. That's because the brain knows it will be called on for the facts later, so it is more careful to heed and hold onto it. This is the true benefit of retrieval. Over time, you naturally begin to pay attention and remember more without trying or exhorting a great deal of effort. The technique continually builds on itself the more you use it.

The best thing about retrieval is that it doesn't require much from you. Like repetition, retrieval doesn't entail developing a new skill, learning a complicated process, or acquiring a new routine. Nor do you need note-taking instruments like pen and paper, learning materials like books and notes, or to be in front of a desk, computer, or phone. In fact, retrieval requires nothing.

All you need is to be with your thoughts and think about and call to mind as much detail of whatever you want or are trying to remember. That means this exercise can be done anytime and anywhere, whether waiting in line, stuck in traffic, on the train, in the shower, cooking, cleaning, walking, or even while driving. Fit the exercise in between parts of the day where you are not doing anything anyway.

In summary, retrieval is the simplest, most powerful memory tool, and it works on a wide range of information. As numerous studies have shown, it works better than using multiple techniques.

Still, you must use it to reap the benefits, so don't let the technique slide under the radar. Apply it in all areas of your life, whether it's to a conversation you had, a story you read, a movie you watched, a podcast you heard, advice you received, an incident that occurred, the reaction you felt, or an event you experienced. Even the associations you learned in the previous chapter will require the use of retrieval to retain, so get into the habit of practicing retrieval all the time and everywhere.

I recommend starting now. Recall what you just read in this chapter or what you have learned so far in this book. If you are not able to recall the material, there is a good chance you won't remember it when you need to apply it. So, practice the technique right now with this chapter and see how much you remember. Can you recall the tips offered or how about the examples that were provided?

CHAPTER SEVEN - IMAGINE THAT!

The image is more than an idea. It is a vortex or cluster of fused ideas and is endowed with energy—Ezra Pound

Visualization is the act of creating a mental image. It is using the imagination to sketch a picture, scene, or process in the mind. For instance, everyone knows what a turtle looks like. Most can also identify the color yellow. Now, if you were to imagine a "yellow turtle," you would be using the power of visualization.

Visualization is a key element in memory because the mind is a visual machine. It thinks not only in words, but also in pictures. When you have a thought or idea, images run in the background to make sense of that thought. When providing directions to a location, you do so from the image of the neighborhood that exists in your mind. Most, if not all, of your thoughts are connected to mental images in some way—even if you are not consciously aware of them.

What's more, the mind processes images far better than words. If you look at a picture of a pine tree, your mind can take the entire image and instantly understand it as a tree. The same is true when recognizing a face. When looking at a friend, your mind doesn't study each individual feature such as the eyes, ears, nose, and wrinkles to conclude that the person before you is a friend. The image is taken as a whole, and the connection is made immediately.

On the other hand, looking at a verbal description of a pine tree or of your friend would take much longer to read the description, digest the information, and make sense of the words. Also, a long and descriptive narrative would be required to clearly convey the image. Without a doubt, images are faster and easier to process than words.

Not only does the mind process images better, it stores and recalls them better as well. Thinking back to your childhood, you will notice all those memories are visual. Running off to school, playing with friends, enjoying holidays with family, as well as the major events of your youth are remembered as crystal-clear images. They are neither stored nor recalled as verbal descriptions.

To demonstrate further, think about the various homes you've lived in over the years. The images of these places appear easily, including details of the living room, dining room, backyard, and immediate neighborhood. However, recalling the address or phone number of these places may not occur as easily. The same is true with people. It is easy to recognize a person's face, but not so easy to recall their name. You never hear anyone say, "Oh, I know your name, but I don't recognize your face."

It is for this reason that the saying, "A picture is worth a thousand words" is so true. Since pictures are worth a thousand words, in essence, you can understand and memorize a thousand words worth of information with mental images. Using visualization to create pictures in your mind of material you want to remember allows you to process, store, and recall information with far more clarity than mere words. The technique provides a level of comprehension not possible any other way.

Visualization can be used to memorize a wide variety of information. Anything you can imagine, you can memorize via visualization. The technique is especially valuable for noting details of a story, processes at work, and instructions from a boss. Let's review how to use visualization in these ways and more.

Story or Novel

From the time we enter kindergarten to the time we graduate college, we are required to read a variety of novels. Whether *A Tale of Two Cities* by Charles Dickens, *Romeo and Juliet* by William

Shakespeare, or even *Green Eggs and Ham* by Dr. Seuss, there is no shortage of literature in our lives.

Even though you may carefully read a book from cover to cover, you may miss important points, confuse characters, or be mystified by the plot. Your eyes see the words, but for some reason the words and meaning the author is trying to convey fails to register. The next thing you know, you've finished reading a sentence, paragraph, or even an entire chapter only to find you have little to no idea what you just read. It is as if your mind left your body and went to la-la land.

Visualization helps maintain attention and retain minute details of written material. The approach is to mentally construct the narrative as the words describe. When the author writes about the characters, picture each character as they are expressed including what they are wearing, how they are acting, and the expressions on their faces. When the author discusses the scenery, imagine it as if you are experiencing it with all your senses. As the plot thickens, picture the events unfolding from one scene to the next. Envision each facet of the novel and make it vivid and visceral, and hence memorable.

To practice, let's explore the *Great Gatsby*, a Jazz Age novel by F. Scott Fitzgerald. In the first chapter, the main character, Nick Caraway, gives the following description of a man named Tom Buchanan:

> …he was a sturdy, straw haired man of thirty with a rather hard mouth and a supercilious manner. Two shining, arrogant eyes had established dominance over his face and gave him the appearance of always leaning aggressively forward. Not even the effeminate swank of his riding clothes could hide the enormous power of that body - he seemed to fill those glistening boots until he strained the top lacing and you could see a great pack of muscle shifting when

his shoulder moved under his thin coat. It was a body
capable of enormous leverage - a cruel body.

Mentally draw the person this description paints—a strong, sturdy
man in his thirties with muscles that show through his coat. He is a
man whose strength is conveyed not just by his physical features but
also the demeanor of *overconfident eyes* and an *aggressive forward
lean*. Picture the thin coat, riding clothes, and glistening boots.

You might even stop reading for a few seconds to form a solid
picture. This way, anytime "Tom" is brought up later in the story,
you are met with a clear vision of how he looks and how he interacts
with others.

Next, practice visualizing a scene in the story:

> Their house was even more elaborate than I expected,
> a cheerful red and white Georgian Colonial mansion
> overlooking the bay. The lawn started at the beach
> and ran toward the front door for a quarter of a mile,
> jumping over sun-dials and brick walks and burning
> gardens - finally when it reached the house drifting up
> the side in bright vines as though from the momentum
> of its run. The front was broken by a line of French
> windows, glowing now with reflected gold, and wide
> open to the warm windy afternoon.

While reading this description, visually construct each aspect of the
location, setting, and scenery. Imagine a red and white colonial style
mansion sitting in front of a lawn that is a quarter mile long and has
sun-dials, brick walkways, and gardens, leading up to a beach.

Add the French windows on the house reflecting gold sunlight from
the sun. Insert each piece to the scene as it is described and really see
it in your mind and not just as something that you read. If don't
know what a Georgian Colonial mansion looks like, search for some
pictures online to understand the setting.

Continue this with all aspects of the story including the major events that take place such as Nick meeting Gatsby, introducing him to Daisy, and then sparking a love affair. Put in your mental picture any and all details that the author takes time to explain, express, and communicate.

To take it one step further, add emotions to the images. Put yourself in the character's shoes and feel what they feel. When Nick hears about Gatsby's death, feel the depth of his loss, his feeling hopeless and unable to do anything to help his friend. Sense his feelings of betrayal when nobody comes to Gatsby's funeral, especially Daisy who was supposedly in love with Gatsby. When he meets Daisy and Tom on the street after he has left New York, feel his anger at how these two people could be so cruel to everyone in the world around them.

Merely reading words does little to aid memory or even concentration. It just doesn't. You can practice repetition, retrieval, and association several times and still not grasp the finer elements until it is visualized. In fact, you may have missed many of the details when initially reading these excerpts from The Great Gatsby.

With visualization, you actively construct the story. Like constructing a house, you take the raw materials and assemble the various elements as they are revealed. This gives the brain a clearer picture of the narrative and that's the picture it records.

Process

In contrast to novels, technical information does not bring with it the luxury of sensory descriptions and emotional interaction. However, visualization can still be applied to illustrate concepts and processes.

If studying the mechanics of a car engine, rather than struggling to memorize a written or verbal description of how each individual part runs and what happens at each step, visualize the process from beginning to end. Picture all the parts working together, from the cycle of air intake aiding fuel injection, to the combustion pushing the pistons, to the crankshaft powering the wheels of the car. Visually seeing the process is going be much more helpful than reading about it.

The body has its own share of processes that can be better explained and remembered via visualization, such as the phases involved in mitosis. Mitosis is the process where a cell divides to form two identical cells that are genetically the same.

To employ visualization, first, picture the nucleus of the cell shrink and disappear. Then see the chromosomes line up along the middle of the cell. Next, the chromosomes divide into two identical pairs and are pulled to the opposite ends of the cells.

After, draw new nuclei around the chromosomes on each side. Finally, see the main cell divide into two distinct cells, each containing the same number and kind of chromosomes as the original cell. It might help to Google images or videos of the process to really nail down the imagery.

Can this technique be applied at work?

Yes, it can.

Suppose you need to remember how products are manufactured at your new job. Simple. Visualize the routine from beginning to end. Picture raw materials arriving at the company through numerous vendors. You might even imagine each vendor loading textile onto trucks for delivery.

Then imagine the materials arriving at the facility and going through production. See each phase in detail as the product moves through various stages of assembly to the final stage of inspection. Lastly, picture the products leaving production and shipping out to customers.

This technique can be applied to any process, cycle, or system. Simply take the various stages involved in a process and visualize how each stage advances from one to the next. To recall the information, simply call up the images you visualized. You'll find those images materialize more quickly and easily than any words ever will.

When employing the technique, add as much detail as possible. You can expand the image to view how the individual components operate or shrink it to see how those components come together as a whole. You can even flip and rotate the image to view the various angles. The more you add to the mental image, the more you will retain.

You can even add personal touches at each stage or concept. Consider studying computer networking, and more specifically, how nodes send and receive encrypted data. You might imagine the sending node to be yourself and the receiving node to be your significant other. The packet of information might be a love letter written in a special code decipherable only by the recipient.

Attaching personal touches in this way invites the power of association to connect the technical topic to something more meaningful, thus engraving the concept deeper. The more meaningful and personal the images, the higher chance they stay strong.

One of the reasons visualization is so effective with processes is because it aids comprehension. It allows you to understand all of the inner workings, and as you learned in Chapter 4, comprehension is extremely important for memorization. Comprehension aids the mind in making the appropriate connections for storage. With gaps or holes in understanding, the mind won't know how to interpret the data, making it difficult to record. Use visualization to fill in those holes.

Instructions

In addition to stories, novels, and processes, visualization is fantastic for memorizing instructions, which usually involve a series of steps. Instructions can prove challenging because in addition to remembering each item in the series, one must remember the order in which they are performed.

The way to do this is to take a set of instructions and picture yourself performing them as directed. If following instructions on a new software, mentally perform each step. When told to open a file, picture yourself opening the file. When instructed to enter data, see yourself enter the text as described. Witness yourself perform each step from start to finish.

As you learned in Chapter 1, repetition is one of the best ways to remember tasks. Think of visualizing instructions as a form of repetition referred to as *mental* practice, as the practice takes place inside your mind. Studies show mental practice is just as effective, if not more, in not only learning new tasks, but also performing them well. Top performers in every field attest to the amazing benefits that mental practice has on their performance. Through visualization, a person can both remember and perform instructions at a high level.

Lists

Another application of visualization deals with remembering an inventory of items, like a grocery list. The application is as straightforward as the previous suggestions–simply take each item on the list and picture it in your mind.

Suppose you are driving home from work, and suddenly remember the need to stop at the store to pick up the following groceries: green tomatoes, ripened bananas, loaf of bread, gallon of milk, brick of cheese, stick of butter, pound of sliced roast beef, and a dozen drumsticks. You can approach remembering this list in one of several ways.

One way is to picture each item stacked on top of one other. Imagine ripened bananas resting on top of green tomatoes. On top of the bananas, picture a loaf of bread. On top of the bread, see the gallon of milk, and so on until every item is included in the image. This is a quick and dirty way to remember a list with each item acting as a cue for those above and below. Once at the store, simply refer to the image to recall the items.

A variation is to visualize the items rolling into and striking each other. Imagine a green tomato rolling down a bowling lane and striking a series of bananas, causing them to tumble and bump the bread. The bread loaf then slides into the milk, which topples and spills onto the brick of cheese, and on and on. This is the same list, but approached differently.

To take the exercise one step further, imagine yourself at the store, rolling the cart to the products. Now picture grabbing each one from the shelf, and placing it in the cart. See the exact brand, size, and color you wish to remember to buy. Once you arrive at the store, use the visual sequence to steer you through the aisles until the list is complete.

On the Fly

The last application of visualization involves using it in the moment to remember important details or pertinent reminders. You are working diligently when the boss stops by your desk to notify that the report deadline has been moved up to 2:00 p.m. She also announces that eight copies need to be delivered to the conference room on the sixth floor.

After repeating the instructions back to her, briefly take a moment and picture the hour hand on your watch at the 2:00 position, you just finished the report and are now walking to the copier and hitting the "8" button to make eight copies. Afterwards, picture an image of you walking to the conference room to deliver said copies. Going through this quick sequence instantly pins the instructions in mind, increasing the likelihood of following through on them.

In another instance, while driving the kids to school, a thought pops in your mind to stop at the cleaners. As soon as the reminder arises, quickly create a mental sequence of you dropping the kids off to school and then driving straight to the cleaners. More often than not, you'll find, without another reminder, you perform the visualized action. It just happens. The mind naturally guides us in the direction of our mental pictures.

Although it helps to close your eyes when visualizing, it's not necessary. As mentioned in the introduction of this chapters, mental images are running in the background all the time. So, it is possible to quickly run through the sequence with eyes wide open, even when driving. Just make sure to do it quickly and not get distracted by the image.

With Other Techniques

The great thing about visualization is that it plays well with other memory techniques. If you enjoy the association method discussed in Chapter 5, you can visualize any association you create. If you are associating birds to their respective State, for instance, visualize the two together.

Visualization also works great with retrieval. To recall the details of a specific moment in my day, I often close my eyes and picture myself in the situation where I learned, heard, or came across the material. For instance, to elicit a conversation I had with a friend at a café last week, I will picture my friend and I back at the café, sitting in the same seats.

Just by forming the image of us at the café, I am able to recall the conversation in exquisite detail. I don't have to strain to think about the fine points, they instantly come to me. Visualizing our get together triggers all sorts of memories of the event and everything that was said or occurred.

Combining visualization with retrieval can be used other ways, for example, to remember answers during an exam. Anytime you are stuck on a question, close your eyes and picture yourself back in class the day the teacher discussed that topic. Try seeing the writing on the white board or the teacher explaining the material. If the answer doesn't come up immediately, steer the image by going to moments that you do remember and noticing the additional details that spring forth. If you remember a classmate raising his hand, picture that and see what other thoughts arise.

These are just a few of the many ways to apply visualization day to day. It is a powerful technique akin to photographic memory. Individuals with photographic memory are able to remember and recall events, experiences, and data with extreme precision. In fact, such individuals can regurgitate pages of text with a single glance.

They can to do this because their mind takes photographic images of the information, and when they need to recall the details, they refer to the image their mind captured. These individuals report seeing the illustration in their head and their eyes appear to scan across the mental copy as they pull the descriptions from it.

This process is similar to what you do with visualization. You capture images of information you want to remember and then reference those images to recall the essential details. The main difference between this technique and photographic memory is that the skill of photographic memory is a natural process for those who have it. They didn't learn to do it nor do they actively think about doing it. Their mind innately does it for them.

Even though this is an innate skill to some, it is possible to cultivate and refine it in yourself. You may not reach the level of a master memorizer, recalling an entire page of text with a single glance, but you can reap 90 percent of the benefits of photographic memory by applying the suggestions in this chapter.

Though the technique requires practice to refine. In the beginning, you may experience difficulty bringing the mental images into clear focus or experience the mind throwing details into the copy that you don't want. In some cases, you may not be able to keep attention on the image, finding that after a few moments the mind has moved on to a completely different thought.

These difficulties are normal, especially in the beginning. With practice, your skills will improve, and as they improve, visualization will become more natural. It may take time, effort, and dedication, but you will get there. I know you will.

CHAPTER EIGHT - TELL ME A STORY

Storytelling is the most powerful way to put ideas into the world today—Robert McKee

Humans are drawn to stories. We watch movies, read novels, listen to music, and attend plays—all of which tell a story. Journalists use storytelling to report the news. Lawyers use them to express their client's voice. Religions weave stories into their message, and there are even stories behind toys and video games. Stories play an important part in our lives.

What's more, the mind is built to remember information delivered through stories. Long before there was television, radio, theatre, or even writing, humans passed on knowledge through story telling. It's how our ancestors trained, coached, educated, and shared important life lessons. More importantly, such tales were the only means to pass on tradition and values across generations. Over time, our brains became wired to engage, retain, and access information through story.

In fact, research shows that the human brain more readily retains information and concepts when presented in story form. That's because stories contain all of the previously discussed elements essential for memory.

Stories put information into a meaningful context so it can be easily associated to other information. They activate the visual senses as the narrative plays out in our head. They engage the auditory senses as the story is heard. Furthermore, stories stimulate the emotions, making the information engaging, and thus, easier to pay attention to. Stories put the whole brain to work.

So how can you put storytelling to work for you? For starter, learn the story behind important names, dates, facts, definitions, and events. Instead of merely receiving a fact, study the story behind its origin. Most everything has some sort of interesting account behind it.

For instance, Chapter 5 discussed that the Serbian assassination of Austria-Hungarian Archduke Franz J. Ferdinand was the spark that ignited World War I. The Archduke was shot by Serbian Nationalist Gavrilo Princip. To preserve these facts, learn the story behind the assassination.

The initial plan to kill Franz Ferdinand wasn't to use a gun at all, but rather a bomb. Also, Princip wasn't the main assassin or even the first option. There were seven assassins strategically lined up along a street in Sarajevo where the Archduke's car was scheduled to pass.

The first two assassins failed to act out of fear. The third threw a bomb, but it bounced off the convertible cover of the Archduke's car and exploded under the vehicle behind it. The fourth, fifth, and sixth in line saw the explosion and assumed the assassination was a success, so they fled. As the bomb went off, Ferdinand's procession sped off so quickly that the remaining conspirator, Gavrilo Princip, didn't have time to act.

In a coincidental turn of events, Franz Ferdinand narrowly escaped a string of assassins and was alive and well at the Town Hall. Meanwhile, Gavrilo Princip sat at a café, upset and ashamed for failing his mission. This could have been the end of the story, but…

Franz Ferdinand decided to get back in his car and head toward the hospital to visit the wounded from the bombing. His driver made a wrong turn, and guess where that turn led?

Right to Gavrilo Princip!

The assassin couldn't believe his luck as the Archduke's car stopped right where he was standing. The rest is "history" as Princip pulled out his gun and shot Archduke Ferdinand from five feet away, sparking a chain of events that led to one of the greatest wars in human history.

This is a great example of how the story behind a fact or historical date can make the date memorable. This account paints a clear picture of the events surrounding the assassination, making it interesting enough to not only pay attention, but to lock down.

Stories are fairly easy to interlace into historical information, but how can this be done with other types of facts? Suppose you're studying geography and learn that Canberra is the capital of Australia. Naturally, one would assume Sydney or Melbourne to be the capital since those are the largest cities in Australia, and generally, the largest city of a country is the capital. So how did such a small and unfamiliar city like Canberra become capital?

Well, the story goes…

When Australia was deciding on a capital, both Sydney and Melbourne fought for the title. Due to a long-standing rivalry between the two cities, neither let up. To appease both sides, Canberra, a city halfway between Sydney and Melbourne, was chosen.

A separate state was even created for Canberra so that it wouldn't be part of either the state of Sydney (New South Wales) or Melbourne (Victoria). Even though neither city was chosen, to this day a friendly rivalry still exists between the two. Clearly, the intriguing story behind Australia's choice for its capital makes the fact painless to keep straight.

Recalling stories written or told by others is one way to use storytelling to enhance memory. Another is to make up a story that weaves together information or items one hopes to conserve. For example, to record a list, create a narrative that incorporates each item or entry from the list. The tale does not have to be long or complex. Just make sure that everything in the list is included in the story. It helps to tie together the sequence of events so that recalling one item leads to the recall of the next.

To demonstrate, pretend you need to visit the hardware store to purchase the following items: hammer, galvanized nails, fluorescent light bulbs, a bristle tip paint brush, a six-foot extension cord, and a space heater. Consider the following story as one option:

> A nail is running because an angry hammer wants to strike it into the ground. The nail sees some fluorescent light bulbs and hides between them, knowing the hammer won't strike the bulbs or they will break. Instead, the hammer calls the bristle tip paint brush to sweep out the nail. As the nail is swept out, it grabs an extension cord and makes a harrowing escape by swinging onto a space heater 6 feet away.

Such a story can be created to remember the grocery list presented in Chapter 7.

> It begins with a tomato sailing on a banana. Once the banana lands on shore, the tomato jumps off and hops on a loaf of bread. The loaf gallops to the laundry detergent to clean itself and so on. This takes the component of an image and adds a story to it.

One can even create a story to archive the list of elements in the periodic table. The first six elements, in order of atomic number, are hydrogen, helium, lithium, beryllium, boron, and carbon. The story might unfold as follows:

> A "hydrogen" bomb is about to detonate in London, but luckily it is flown away by "helium" balloons. You take pictures of the balloons with your "lithium"

battery powered camera and send them to your friend "Beryl Lium." In excitement, your friend trips over his cat "Boron." Everyone celebrates this historic day with a barbeque using "carbon" coals.

Such a story makes it simple to recite the elements and in the correct order. It's possible to extend the story to the remaining elements such as nitrogen, oxygen, and beyond.

The tales you create don't need to be elaborate, complex, or overly detailed. The narrative can be simple like Hemmingway's six-word piece "For sale: Baby shoes, Never worn." Also, the technique doesn't have to be reserved for complex subjects like the periodic table. They can be used to remember something as simple as a license plate. To mentally store the following license plate, MF 105, you might create a simple story like, '*Hot day in Miami, Florida, 105 degrees.*

Naturally, other options exist. The sillier and more extravagant, the better. A certain degree of clever fun makes the story stick.

CHAPTER NINE - CLUSTERS

You cannot eat a cluster of grapes at once, but it is very easy if you eat them one by one—Jacques Roumain

As discussed in Chapter 5, tools like acronyms and acrostics associate information to other information giving the brain more access to that information. A concept similar to acronyms and acrostic is clustering.

Clustering is a method of breaking long pieces of information into smaller groups. A phone number in the United States uses a very specific pattern of clustering like in the number (312) 329-4431. The numbers are grouped into 3 clusters, and no one cluster is more than four digits long. Grouping numbers like this is far easier to retain than "3123294431."

Clustering works not just with numbers, but also words. Trying to summon the spelling of the word "supercalifragilisticexpialidocious" from the Disney movie *Mary Poppins* is a monster that makes the eyes glaze over with disinterest or even dread.

However, dividing the word into smaller clusters instantly makes the word easier to conquer. First, learn "super," then "cali," "fragi," "listic," "expi," "ali," and finally, "docious." It's not so daunting in such small, manageable pieces. Simply study the smaller bits and then put them together.

With words, it helps to cluster by the syllables in the pronunciation. In the previous example, the word was clustered every two syllables: "ca-li," "fra-gi," and "lis-tic." Such two-syllable sounds are far easier to pronounce and learn. Once each part is divided, say them out loud several times in sequence, going faster with each pass. By increasing speed, the individual clusters merge into one whole word.

In addition to remembering numbers and words, clusters can also be used with lists. The following to-do list includes the tasks "wash car, clean bathroom, draft proposal, exercise, change oil, do laundry, replace car tires, finish sales report, pick up kids, reply to emails, vacuum living room, buy groceries, call back client, throw out trash, and drop off mail." As is, this list looks like a string of words that can hypnotize the mind, so items will undoubtedly be forgotten.

Breaking the same list into smaller groups or clusters, however, proves far easier. Start by looking at all the items in the list. Then, think of meaningful groups into which you can cluster the items. The goal is to group each item into some sort of logical or common-sense categories. The following is one way the previous list of items can be grouped:

Household Chores—clean bathroom, do laundry, vacuum living room, throw out trash

Work-Related Tasks—draft proposal, finish sales report, respond to employee emails, call back client

Car-Related Tasks—wash car, change oil, replace tires

Outside Activities—exercise, pick up kids, buy groceries, drop-off mail

The new list takes the long inventory of items and puts them into smaller groupings. All items are placed in one of the shorter categories, and not only are the smaller groupings easier to remember, but they are also better organized.

This can be done to remember a variety of lists. Again, all that's required is to think about the high-level categories and then arrange each item into those categories or "clusters."

Understanding Your Digital Capacity

In 1956, psychologist George Miller published his groundbreaking work on mental digit span. This is the capacity of the mind to hold digits in conscious memory, the portion of memory discussed in Chapter 1 used to retain new pieces of information.

Studies reveal that if dots are flashed on a screen and a person is asked how many dots were shown, they begin making errors at around seven dots. With fewer dots, a person can accurately count them. With a quantity greater than seven, people seem to resort to guessing.

Seven digits or distinct pieces of information seems to be the most we can comfortably hold in our conscious awareness. This is the reason phone numbers in the United States are limited to seven digits as it is the largest cluster for most people. Clusters of three and four digits are far simpler, and that's why phone numbers are clustered even further as in 329-4431.

By knowing this natural limitation, you can cluster information into groups of no more than seven items. That is, if you are going to break long numbers, words, and lists into smaller groups or categories, it helps to limit each group to about 6 or 7 items.

There are exceptions to this limit. Some people have been known to work past nine digits, while others are strapped with as little as five, but most people find seven a comfortable maximum. Determine your maximum and work within it. The other option is to…

Increase Your Digit Span

One of the best ways to enhance memory is by increasing digit span. As much as 50% of the disparity in intelligence among people comes from the previously mentioned variation in conscious memory or digit limit. To put it another way, the larger a person's conscious capacity, the higher his or her IQ. By increasing digit span, you can not only improve memory, but may end up increasing intelligence as well.

There is an easy technique to increase digit span. Take a string of numbers, and then from memory, try to recall the string in reverse order. In other words, glance at a number, then hide the number and write the reverse of that number on a separate piece of paper. For instance, if the first number is 4971, write down 1794.

Start with numbers with low digit counts, like three or four digits. Write down a series of numbers with that digit span. Peek at the first number, and without looking at it again, write on a separate piece of paper the number in reverse. Then do that for the second number. Keep practicing with a certain digit count until you gain comfort with it.

The object is then to move to higher counts. Be sure to master each digit count before moving on to the next higher quantity. When you get to a count that proves difficult, stay with that digit span until it becomes easy to recall backwards. Majority of the memory-boosting benefits stop at between nine to eleven digits, so you can stop at these quantities (unless you just want to prove you can do more).

At initial glance, expanding digit count doesn't seem all that beneficial. It is hard to imagine how being able to recall strings of meaningless numbers can have any sort of impact on memory. Well, the foundation of every mental task relies on a person's ability to hold a series of items in the mind and process it in sequential order, one after another.

Take the simple act of tying shoe laces, which requires not only knowing all of the steps, but also knowing what step you are on, which step is next, and the one after that. If you cannot keep track of the steps and the correct order, what seems like a simple task would be impossible. This applies to any task like taking a series of words to form a sentence, a string of notes to play a song, or a set of directions to find a destination.

More importantly, all higher-level mental functions require lower level skills because lower level skills are the building blocks of those higher-level tasks. The more complex a task is, the more it relies on low-level skills such as the ability to process sequential order of numbers. So even though digit span is a low-level skill, by developing and enhancing it, you in turn develop and enhance performance of high-level tasks.

With that said, spending 10 minutes a day on expanding digit count will significantly improve memory and cognitive abilities. If you find numbers boring, substitute numbers with shapes, colors, animals, or any other object to make it enjoyable. For example, create a list of shapes and then try to draw the list in reverse order. Or, look at a series of colors and then recall the series backwards. Switching things up like this can make the exercise more engaging.

This wraps up clustering. Breaking a large or long list of items down into manageable chunks or clusters makes for easier recall. Keep the size of the cluster within your digital limit or expand that limit to enhance both memory and intelligence.

CHAPTER TEN - TAKE NOTE!

He listens well who takes notes—Dante

Most of the memory techniques discussed so far involve activities that can be performed without the aid of other material. However, one of the most reliable memory techniques is one that requires at least a pen and paper.

Note taking is the act of writing down anything you want to recall later. You transcribe information in a notebook, tablet, sticky pad, or just about anywhere, and as long as the information is transcribed correctly, you can refer to it whenever you need, wherever you need, and as many times as you need.

With notes, there are no techniques to apply or systems to remember, and the content does not dwindle or fade away. It will always be there as long as you don't delete, throw away, or lose the note.

The problem with note taking is that it is impossible to carry around all your notes, all of the time. If you had in your pocket every piece of information you wanted to bear, your pants would be the size of a mainframe computer.

Additionally, it would be time consuming to sort through everything to find the exact piece of information in the exact moment. Even worse, if you misplaced the notes, you would be at a total loss.

That is why the techniques in this book are so vital. They help you store and recall essential information without the use of a portable mainframe, while allowing quicker access.

While the techniques in this book reduce the need for a portable mainframe, taking notes is nonetheless a powerful way to strengthen memory. Countless studies show that people who take notes, whether of a lecture, book, or even a to-do list, understand the content better and remember it longer.

Studies also show that even if you never review those notes, the information is still retained better and for longer than if you hadn't taken them in the first place.

That's pretty profound.

So profound in fact, it is worth repeating.

The mere act of taking notes helps one understand information better and for longer, even if those notes are never looked at again!

I'm sure you have experienced this on numerous occasions. You write out a grocery list, a set of directions, or a series of instructions, only to find that you don't need to look at the list, direction, or instructions.

There are several reasons why that is. First and foremost, taking the time to write information signals to the brain that it is something important and worthwhile.

Second, note taking requires paying attention. In a dull lecture or when reading complicated text, the mind has the tendency to wander, especially if the subject is tedious and repetitive. You could be reading and listening for hours on end and not have a single idea enter awareness.

Taking notes keeps the mind from wandering because one must concentrate on the words, at least to some degree, to be able to not only write ideas down, but to determine which ones are important and noteworthy. As stated in Chapter 2, concentration is critical for memory.

Third, the act of having pen and paper in hand ready to write activates the mind to receive information. You don't have to push yourself in anyway, it's a byproduct of being ready to write. You'll be surprised just how much engagement increases by simply being intentional about taking notes.

Lastly, notetaking allows you to process information coming at you. Instead of thoughts and ideas entering and leaving your awareness, like water in a stream, you put the brakes just long enough to digest what's coming in. You begin to see main points and overarching ideas more clearly, as well as the links and relationships between those ideas. As a result, information connects better and is better understood.

Unfortunately, note-taking has many stigmas and misconceptions. Some believe that it is not effective, takes too much time, or a sign that a person has bad memory, Other's believe it to be an archaic process that makes one appear nerdy or "uncool."

The reality is some of the brightest, most successful, and respected people in the world are proponents of note taking. Richard Branson, high profile billionaire and founder of Virgin Group, which controls more than 400 companies around the globe, says that notetaking is his most important habit.

Branson asserts, "I go through dozens of notebooks every year and write down everything that occurs to me each day, an idea not written down is an idea lost." He goes as far as to claim that many of Virgin's companies and projects would never have started without notes.

While Branson is regarded as a "lone wolf," breaking boundaries in his business ventures, he is not alone in this practice. Thomas Edison, Bill Gates, George Lucas, Tim Ferris, Ernest Hemingway, Mark Twain, Pablo Picasso, Sheryl Sandberg, and J.K. Rowling are all notable notetakers. In fact, it is believed Thomas Edison captured over 5 million pages of notes during his life.

Even Brian Tracy, celebrated coach and author of numerous goal setting books, stresses the importance of noting goals. His and others' research reveal that individuals who regularly write down their goals achieve those goals at a considerably higher rate than those who do not.

There is a lot of power in note taking, and much of that power is achieved through improved memory. By remembering what you want or need to do, like these notable men and women, you are more likely to do it. Since we forget 80% of what we hear, see, and learn within a few hours, it's silly to think there is no need for note taking in our lives.

So as much as you may be seeking a fancy or decorative memory technique, one as simple, basic, and archaic as notetaking is often the best solution. As mentioned, it forces focus, encourages engagement, aids processing of information, but more importantly, gives you something to refer to later.

Therefore, instead of trying to evolve from note-taking, your goal should instead be to evolve the note-taking itself. In this day and age, technology has made it easier to capture, review, and share notes. Cellphones, laptops, online calendars, and note-taking software and applications like OneNote or Evernote have made it simpler than ever to jot, preserve, and carry important information. Use these tools to keep up with the pace of technology.

As to the how-to of note taking, there are as many ways to jot notes as there are memory techniques. The strategy depends on what you want to memorize, how the information is delivered, and how you will use the information. It also depends on the person taking the notes and their situation, whether it's a student in class, a professional in a meeting, a contractor at a construction site, or a therapist trying to understand a patient.

Although there is no one prescribed note-taking method, two general approaches exist. One is to summarize information down to short phrases and keywords. The other option is to write down as much as possible, almost verbatim.

Obviously summarizing content down to the essential point is quicker, though such summaries leave little to stimulate recall later. Summarizing the sentence "Interstellar gas is concentrated in an extremely narrow layer close to the galaxy's plane of symmetry," with the following phrase "I.S. gas, narrow layer, plane of symmetry" strips the core of the communication. With hour after hour, and thus page after page of material in any one sitting, going back to review the summarized version may not yield the original meaning.

Writing everything down too has its own disadvantages. It shifts focus from reading, listening, and processing material to simply transcribing. Although this approach ensures that more detail will be available later, in the moment, it's difficult to make sense of the next sentence, thought, or point the speaker is making. When diligently transcribing, it's also difficult to grasp the big picture or the overall points that are made. You have to rely on reviewing the notes to grasp everything and hope that you have written fast enough to ensure everything is recorded.

Regrettably, neither extremes are effective.

The key is balance.

Write as much as possible while still paying attention to the big picture, major points, and main ideas. In other words, simultaneously focus and note as much of the relevant aspects of that communication.

A great way to do this is with the use of shorthand. Shorthand is a method that allows a person to speed up notetaking by substituting letters, abbreviations, or symbols in place of longer words or phrases. For instance, instead of writing out every letter in the word "between," cut it down to "b/t" or reducing the word "number" to the symbol "#." Shorthand drastically reduces the amount of time required to take notes while increasing the detail and clarity.

There are many ways to employ shorthand. One is to use just the beginning of the word, as the following demonstrate:

• pol–politics

• gov–government

• subj–subject

• info–information

• intro–introduction

Another is to use the beginning of a word with the final letter. Some prefer to add an apostrophe (') before the final letter as shown:

• govt–government

• interl–international

• gov't–government

• inter'l–international

Notice in these examples, the shortened words contain less than half the letters than the original. This effectively doubles or triples note-taking speed.

Another option is to omit vowels from the middle of the word, though this only works well when there are consonants in between the vowels:

- prblm–problem

- schl–school

- bkgd–background

Another pattern is to use "g" to represent "ing" endings:

- dcrg–decreasing

- chkg–checking

- estbg–establishing

- exptg–expecting

Never spell out numbers. Instead of writing "one," "two," "three," use their digit equivalent (1, 2, 3). This can be tricky if you see the numbers spelled out because the natural inclination is to copy what is seen. Time is also saved by omitting articles such as "a," "an," and "the."

One of the best ways to reduce writing time is to adopt symbols, which can replace an entire word or phrase with just a few strokes:

= – equal to, the same as

≈ – approximately, similar to

> – greater than

< – less than

– number

$ – money

The following table offers symbols and abbreviations for commonly used words and phrases. Spend some time to memorize them now as they will save considerable time and effort in the future.

Symbol	Meaning	Abbreviation	Definition
→	leads to, causes, shows result	411	information
←	caused by, because of, shows reason	2nte	tonight
↑	increase, more, go up, up, grow	am / pm	morning / evening night
↑↑	rapid increase	admin	administration
↓	decrease, less, go down, down	aka	also known as
↓↓	rapid decrease	assoc	association
=	equal to, same as	atm	at the moment
≠	not equal to, opposite of, not the same	ave	avenue
≈	approximately, similar to	bibliog	bibliography
>	greater than	biol	biology
>>	much greater than	blvd	boulevard
<	less than	btw	by the way
<<	considerably less than	c&p	copy and paste
±	give or take	chem	chemical
x	times, multiply, multiple	co.	company
÷	divide	cont.	continue, continued
∴	therefore	inc / dec	increase / decrease
" "	ditto (same as above)	dept	department

✓	yes, correct	**diff**	difference
✓✓	definitely, certain, proven	**disc**	describe
/	per (e.g. $50/day)	**dist**	distance
∝	proportional to	**distr**	distribute, distribution, distributed
%	percentage	**div**	dividend, division, divide
& or +	and	**DIY**	do it yourself
#	number	**dob**	birthday, date of birth, born
$	money	**econ**	economy, economics
c	cents	**esp.**	especially
@	at	**est**	estimate
'	minutes/feet	**eta**	estimated time of arrival
"	seconds/inches	**faq**	Frequently Asked Questions
♂	man, men, male	**gal**	gallon
♀	woman, women, female	**govt**	government
1st	first (similarly 2nd, 3rd, 4th, etc.)	**hist**	historian, historical, history
Δ	change	**id**	identification
∞	always, no exceptions	**illus**	illustrate, illustrated
Ø	stop	**info**	information
a/f	after	**lang**	language
b/c	because	**lb / lbs**	pound / pounds
b/f	before	**Ln**	lane
b/h	behind	**max / min**	maximum / minimum
b/l	below	**mbr**	member

b/s	beside	mfr	manufacturer
b/t	between	mkt	market
b/y	beyond	mktg	marketing
c/o	care of	mo/wk/ yr/hr	month/week/ year/hour
e/b	everybody	mph	miles per hour
e/o	everyone	mtg	meeting
e/t	everything	N / S / E / W	North / South / East / West
e/w	everywhere	orig	original, originated
e.g.	for example	pc	computer
ff	following	pg / pgs	page / pages
i/s	instead	phd	doctor
i.e.	that is	pt	pint
s/t	something	qt	quart
s/o	someone	qty	quantity
s/w	somewhere	Rd	road
u/f	useful	ref	reference
w/	with	sect	section
w/i	within	St	street
w/o	without	tba	to be announced
re:	regarding	tbsp	tablespoon
vs	versus, against	tsp	teaspoon
8	anything ending in 'ate'	xchg	exchange
?	uncertain, possibly, unproven	yr/yrs	year/years

You may adapt this list by creating your own abbreviations based on the profession or type of information you come across. In law school, many students use a capital "K" for contract, "p" for plaintiff, and "d" for defendant. In economics "S" refers to supply and "D" to demand. In the end, the notes will be your notes, so generate abbreviations for information specific to you.

These are few ways to reduce the number of letters used on words, and hence, the time and effort spent on writing those words. The trick is to pick a system and stick to it. It's easy to fall into the trap of substituting one abbreviation or symbol for multiple words. For instance, "r/s" can easily refer to "relationship" or "restrict" Using it for both can create confusion and defeat the purpose of shorthand and notetaking altogether. Instead, assign an abbreviation or symbol to one word and use it only for that word.

It was mentioned earlier that even if you never look at the notes you take, you still retain the information better. Nonetheless, review your notes. As the forgetting curve from Chapter 1 illustrates, reviewing notes after taking them boosts memory further. It is the power of repetition in play. The sooner you review the notes after taking them, the better–optimally within an hour.

During review, make sure to clarify points that seem vague, don't quite make sense, or are incomplete. If the review jogs memory of additional information, put it down. Don't look at notes as a one-time activity. Effective note taking involves using the original notes many times to build memory of the content.

Mind Maps

Another approach to note taking for the purpose of enhancing memory is called mind maps. Mind Maps are unconventional from the standard method to which you are accustomed. With mind maps, information is noted not word by word or with sentences, but rather in the form of a diagram with lines branching out from one fact to another. Moreover, unlike standard methods of note taking where a writer starts at the top of the page and works down, mind maps start in the center of the page and branch out like a spider web.

To take notes using mind maps, first place the main subject in the center as the main idea. From the center, branch out with supporting details. This is done by drawing lines out from the center and labeling each with facts or points about the main idea. Next, create secondary branches that support those primary branches, continuing to expand outward with more and more detail as new information is introduced.

Here is an illustration of a mind map:

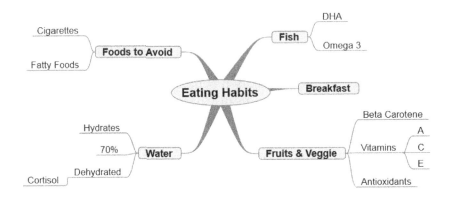

This mind map summarizes the subsection in Chapter 4 discussing eating habits that aid memory. Since the topic is on eating habits, it is placed in the center. In that section, we discussed the importance of breakfast and eating fish, fruits, and vegetables. We also addressed the importance of drinking water and avoiding certain types of foods. So, these points of discussion are recorded as the primary branches.

Within each primary branch, we added supporting facts with secondary branches. The "fruits and veggies" branch lists what was mentioned about their benefits; that they are a good source of beta carotene, vitamins A, C, and E, and antioxidants. The "water" branch reveals the important points about drinking water.

This is a quick description of how to use mind maps. To summarize, begin with the main idea in the center, then radiate outward with supporting and subsidiary details. There are no limits to the number of supporting and subsidiary branches you create.

The illustration above is a basic example, used merely to illustrate the concept, though this system has considerably more potential than the illustration shows. It can manage and organize far more detail to survey, present, arrange, and nail down important data. Below is a different example that highlights just how much detail can be added.

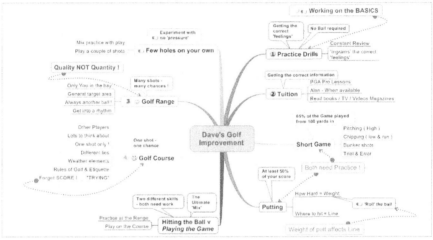

http://www.mind-mapping.co.uk/

This mind map notes strategies for becoming a better golfer. The author of this map added primary branches for the main tactics he plans to use, which include "Practice Drills," "Putting," and "Short Game." Within these points are included points that the golfer wants or needs to remember about each tactic. It is important to note that there are no limits to the number of supporting and subsidiary branches included in a mind map. Add as many points as necessary.

Noting information using mind maps has many benefits. For starters, such notes are more visual, and as we discussed in Chapter 7, visual information is easier to remember. Mind maps also help one to develop clear associations between ideas, and as explained in Chapter 5, associations are fundamental to memory. More importantly, notes taken this way organize and structure information better, in turn making the information easier to understand, and recalling from Chapter 4, comprehension is a key aspect of memory.

Mind maps are useful for more than note taking. The tool is also great for studying, brainstorming, planning, and writing. Mind Maps: Quicker Notes, Better Memory, and Improved Learning 3.0 is an excellent resource that will get you up to speed about the benefits of mind maps and how to apply them in these areas and beyond.

CHAPTER ELEVEN - MORE MEMORY POWER TOOLS

A determined soul will do more with a rusty monkey wrench than a loafer will accomplish with all the tools in a machine shop—Robert Hughes

While this book has presented many memory tools, there are still more to explore. This chapter uncovers five additional techniques to help you understand, store, and recall.

Getting Organized

One memory improvement activity people overlook is getting organized. Disorganization increases the number of places to put things, be it paper that needs to be filed or bills that need to be paid, and hence, more places where things can be forgotten. If there are piles of paper on a coffee table, dining table, kitchen table, on the bed, and in the car, then there are that many more areas where documents can be left and that many more areas to search when a document has gone missing.

The same goes for other articles such as clothes, garbage, and boxes. The more items laying around the house, the more locations the mind has to categorize and search when those articles go missing. This clutters the mind, causing it to be less focused and more distracted.

On the other hand, when you are organized, you have a system for where things belong. Dirty clothes go in the hamper, letters in the drawer, books on the shelf, and so on. With a system like this, there is no mess to remember. All that is required is to remember the system. When searching for an important letter, you know to look in the drawer because that is where letters go. There is no need to search on top, in between, and under piles everywhere.

Here are some effective strategies for getting organized.

Assign places to put things - As Rosie, the futuristic robot from the iconic animated sitcom *The Jetsons* uttered, there is "a place for everything and everything in its place." Meaning, every item should have a spot where it can be stored and should be neatly returned to that spot when not in use. Keep phone numbers in an address book, keys in the front hall, and ID's in a wallet or a purse. Assign a place for all the items, so you know where to look when they are needed.

Avoid paper piles—There are generally two things that happen to information buried in a paper pile—either it is forgotten, or as mentioned, it can't be found when needed. To avoid paper piles, do one of the following when receiving documents:

1. File it to its assigned place.

2. Write the information down elsewhere (such as in a scheduler) and toss it.

3. Simply toss it.

Another way to avoid paper piles is to steer clear of using sticky notes or other small note pads. If you need to write or note something, do so in a notebook, calendar, or smart phone. While it's okay to use a reminder such as a sticky note every once in a while, using such notes all the time makes them less noticeable, and as a result, less useful.

Tidy up often—The difficulty with organization lies not in the initial act of getting organized, but rather in the continuous act of staying that way. People often fail with organizing because after getting organized, they don't put in the effort needed to keep things tidy. They slowly let things slip, allowing clutter to seep back in, as piles once again build.

With that said, don't let too many hours or days go by in between straightening up. If you find yourself slipping, make sure to step back and quickly get things in order again. It helps to keep the system as simple as possible. Alphabetize wherever possible, color code items, and label everything clearly and boldly.

Organize Your Time—In addition to organizing space, it helps memory to organize time. Organize time in the same way that you organize space, by assigning times for specific chores, assignments, and activities. This means setting precise schedules for running specific errand.

For example, use mornings before school as a workout time, evenings after work to check the mail, and after dinner to take out the garbage. Set Sunday afternoons as the time for grocery shopping, and for paying bills, consider the first or last day of the month.

As each day approaches, you are automatically reminded what is on tap in terms of chores or time-sensitive tasks. Organizing space will help you remember where to put things, while organizing time will help you remember when to do them.

Forget-Me-Not Spot

Most of us have at one time or another lost our keys, glasses, checkbook, or that memo we had just a second ago. Have you ever stopped to think about why we misplace these items so often? Usually it's because we aren't paying attention when we put them down.

We're distracted, so putting something down is not what we're focused on. We might be distracted by a call from our boss, the door bell ringing, or the kids making a mess. Misplacing things has nothing to do with how old we are—only with how preoccupied the mind is.

How can we keep from losing things we need and thus save unnecessary aggravation, not to mention wasted time that goes along with it? The best way to remember where things are put is always to put them in the same place, referred to as a "forget-me-not spot." By always putting the items we need, such as our keys, glasses, or wallet, in the same place, we don't need to pay attention to where we put them, as they will always be in that forget-me-not spot.

Here are some tips for using a forget-me-not spot.

Pick a convenient place—The forget-me-not spot should be conveniently located so you actually use it. At home, the best place is near the door you enter and exit most frequently. At the office, the best place is most likely somewhere on your desk. It can be a drawer, shelf, bowl, or a box. I once heard about a woman who had a table in her foyer painted with images of her keys, wallet, and glasses. While it probably worked well for her, it's not necessary to go to this extreme.

Pick a place that can hold all your things—The designated forget-me-not spot should be a place that can hold all the items you want to put there. It will also help to have extra room for additional now-and-then articles that need to be remembered, such as a dry-cleaning receipt or a library book that needs to be returned.

Make sure to use your forget-me-not spot—With a forget-me-not-spot, although you don't have to be conscious about *where* you put things, you do have to be conscious to put them in the right place. If you set the coffee table as the "go to" place for keys, then make sure that anytime you place keys, they are placed there. Items can only be found in a set location if they are left in that location. This really is a case of use it or lose it.

It might help to rehearse this action several times. Go outside, enter the front door, walk up to the coffee table, and place your keys in the assigned spot. Pick up the keys, go back outside, walk in and place the keys on the coffee table again. Do this a few more times to ingrain the action both in the mind and muscles.

To reinforce the action, visualize the rehearsal. Close your eyes and picture yourself walking through the front door and placing the keys in the forget-me-not spot. Visualize the sequence in various scenarios and contexts, like coming home after work, a jog, dinner out, or after any other activity away from home. Picture yourself walking in the front door and always putting the keys in the designated spot.

Reinforce Correct Answers

Memory is most successful when correct answers are reinforced. When using flash cards to drill knowledge about a subject, for instance, every time you get the right answer, put the card answer side up and read the answer out loud. This repetition and reading the card reinforces that answer.

As the Ebbinghaus forgetting curve suggests, frequency of reinforcement also determines how well a response will be learned and retained. Reviewing flash cards two or three times in spaced succession can prove far more beneficial than going through the set just once.

A different method of reinforcement involves rewarding yourself for correct answers. This could be a bowl of peanuts with a nut for each right answer (okay, okay—maybe a handful of nuts for each right answer). The brain will work harder to answer questions knowing that a reward is involved.

Punishment for wrong answers is often used, but this actually harms more than it helps. Even though punishment may suppress an incorrect response, it does not necessarily get at the root cause of the incorrect response. That wrong answer may reappear once punishment stops.

Moreover, punishment can become an emotionally disruptive cognitive dissonance in the process of learning and storing information. Take kids who are scolded for making errors while reading. They may become so upset that they produce more errors or they stop reading altogether because of the bad memories associated with the activity. When using reinforcement, make sure to support correct responses instead of punishing yourself for incorrect ones.

Poetry—Rhyme and Rhythm

For longer than written history, poetry has been the go-to memory aid. The technique was vital for keeping memory alive from one generation to the next. Epic poems like the *Iliad* and the *Odyssey*, by the ancient Greek poet Homer, are two classic examples.

Before the invention of writing, a bard would travel around the countryside reciting these and other poems. Not only was this a form of entertainment, it was also a way to teach people about the values and customs of a civilization. This oral tradition continued even after the invention of writing, (hence Shakespeare's nickname of "The Bard") and, in fact, is still something we do today when we listen to music or go see a play or movie.

Bards were important and respected people in ancient times not only because of the knowledge they provided, but also because it was an impressive feat to memorize and recite such lengthy pieces. In written form, *The Iliad* and *The Odyssey* are over 1000 pages. The need to easily recall these epic stories without the aid of notes is part of why they were written as poems–rhythms and rhyme help to make something unique and catchy.

While today, a great deal of poetry is freeform and lacking much structure to its rhythm, before the modern era, poems were typically highly structured with up and down beats and a specific number of syllables per line. These standards were necessary because they aided in retention of the poem and because they added to the apparent beauty of the art form.

How can you benefit from this? Write a poem, why not? Take a subject and find rhymes to associate with it. Make a rap song out of it. Subjects like calculus might even become fun when converted to modern poetry or rap. To create a poem to remember the meaning of the two key symbols in calculus, "d" and long "∫", the first means "a little bit of" and the second means "the sum of." The following poem captures these two ideas:

> *The symbols in calculus*
>
> *Might seem quite miraculous*
>
> *If only you knew that "d"*
>
> *Meant a little bit of what you see,*
>
> *And that the long "S"*
>
> *Means sum of subject's caress.*

Or to inscribe the following ingredients for a recipe: chicken, chicken broth, wild rice, dried apples, walnuts, salt, and pepper, try a rhyme like this:

> *Oh, the chicken swam into the broth.*
>
> *The rice brewed wildly.*
>
> *The apples dried on walnut husks on the salt and pepper sea.*

While this technique requires a bit of creativity and a degree of talent, those who like it, really take to it. They find that it's fun to make up rhymes, and let's face it, if something is fun, we're more likely to use it. Even though you may not find it fun initially, give it a shot. You may end up liking it, and who knows, uncover an unknown talent.

The Loci Method

The loci method combines association with visualization. Over the years, the technique has been referred to by many names such as "memory palace" or "building dungeons." Regardless of the name, the technique is basically the same.

The Loci method dates back to antiquity, because as mentioned earlier, in ancient times, people did not have practical means to take or carry notes so a strong memory was vital. In addition to rhymes, narrators and storytellers were forced to devise other ways to remember songs, poems, and tales. One technique they devised was the loci method. With this method, they were able to deliver lengthy stories, word for word, with remarkable accuracy.

What they did was associate each thought of a story to specific parts of their home. These were called "loci" or places. They associated the beginning thought of a story to the front door, the second thought to the hallway, the third to the living room, and so on.

When the narrator wanted to recite a story, thought for thought, he took a mental tour through the home. Visually "seeing" the front door triggered the first part of the piece. Walking in and "seeing" the second place, the hallway, triggered the next piece, and then on and on to the end of the story. It is from these places, or "loci," that the method got its name.

To apply this method, pick a familiar site with many points that can represent your loci. A typical choice for most people is their home, as it is the most familiar, but a park, office, or even a neighborhood works just as well. Whichever site you select, make sure you know it well and that it has enough places to attach meaningful associations.

After selecting a site, identify individual places or loci within that site. With a home, each room in the house can correspond to a locus, with each piece of furniture in the room offering additional space to associate a though, fact, or idea. With a park, different areas of the park and even different objects within the park, such as trees, benches, swings, or sandboxes, can symbolize a locus.

After identifying all the loci, get accustomed to the site. This is important because the site you use will always remain the same— only the information attached to it will change. A good way to achieve this is to do a mental walk through by visualizing yourself moving from the beginning of the site through each locus or room until reaching the end. Do this a few times so that all the places and their order sink in.

Then, to remember information, connect each piece to the familiar site in the order it needs to be remembered. To memorize a speech like Lincoln's *Gettysburg Address*, connect "Four score and seven years ago our fathers" to the front door, "brought forth on this continent, a new nation," to the hallway, "conceived in Liberty, and dedicated to the proposition" to the living room, and then other parts of the speech to other areas of the home. To recite the speech, take a mental tour to elicit the exact words that were connected to each locus in the house.

In addition to stories and speeches, the loci method can also be used to remember lists or other information in a series or sequence. Again, take the established site, then connect individual parts of the list or series to each locus. To recall the 13 colonial states, attach each state to each locus. To record the list of U.S. presidents, attach the names and images of the president to each location. For a grocery list, assign foods to the location.

A variation is to use parts of your body as the loci. Continuing with the example of a grocery, if you need to buy bananas, tomatoes, ground meat, and bread, place each item on a different part of your body: eyes, nose, ears, and fingers. Repeat this list to yourself several times while touching those spots. That is, to associate bananas to the nose, touch the nose as you say bananas; touch the ears as you say tomatoes.

At the store, simply touch the locus on your body to elicit the item associated with it. This method also works well for recalling keywords on a test or a to-do list and combines mental memory with muscle memory, giving your brain two shots at pulling out the correct answer.

The loci method is an excellent technique that many find useful. As mentioned, it is a method that has been around for centuries. Even though the technique is not as simple to jump into as repetition or retrieval, it is time tested.

This warps up the chapter on additional memory aids. Here you learned five ways to further enhance memory–getting organized, forget-me-not-spots, reinforcing correct answers, rhyme and rhythm, and the loci method.

CHAPTER TWELVE - OVERCOMING FORGETFULNESS

The existence of forgetting has never been proved: We only know that some things don't come to mind when we want them—Friedrich Nietzsche

Have you ever forgotten an important meeting, appointment, or spent countless hours on an assignment only to forget to bring it to school or work? Worse, ever left something of value at a restaurant? It is all too common to forget important dates or leave behind important items.

So far, our efforts have focused on how to place information in our heads, and with the use of memory tools, call it up when needed. However, some information needs to be called up on its own. Meaning, it's one thing to memorize an appointment, but another to be reminded when its date and time have approached. Or you may remember to finish a report, but forget to bring it to the meeting for which it was prepared.

"Forgetting" is the brain's inability to remind us of details like meetings, appointments, and schedules in times or moments when needed. The techniques in the previous chapters are useful for storing information, but not quite useful as a reminder tool. Therefore, this book dedicates an entire chapter to overcoming forgetfulness. The chapter begins by looking at the causes of forgetfulness, and then, how best to overcome them.

Theories to Explain Forgetfulness

There are a number of theories to explain this phenomenon called "forgetting." Perhaps the oldest involves the concept that memory has a natural tendency to decay over time. Though not a perfect analogy, the mind storing memories is a bit like a video camera recording. Looking for a specific event in the past is similar to searching for a scene in video footage. An individual can pick an event, review it in slow motion, fast forward, and even pause or zoom in on a particular detail. Though like videotape, these memories can become brittle with age and lose clarity over time. The image we get back when remembering something is frequently blurry or otherwise imperfect.

An alternative idea deals with relevancy of information. When a piece of information, such as a name or number, is no longer relevant, its importance is downgraded, and the brain shifts resources to more relevant details. To better explain, think of the brain as a bank of computer memory chips. While the brain holds a staggering amount of data, its capacity nonetheless remains finite. To make way for new information, the mind compresses old data in a way that it can be reconstructed, if necessary, at a later date. Thus, data quality suffers, so over time, details can be lost or at least become muddled. The event is still there, but fragments may be missing.

Another concept involves distortion, either in the way the information was originally stored or how it is later retrieved. Since faulty traces in our brain are being accessed, this inaccuracy may result in an altered or "false" memory, or it may even prevent retrieval altogether. For example, a person may find stored information that he or she knows cannot be true, so the mind simply rejects it.

Interference is another reason that adversely affects retrieval. A person at a new job is taught 30 different tasks in a single day. With so much to remember, the last procedure that person learns will have a hard time sticking because the previous 29 procedures interfere with that learning. This is what psychologists refer to as "proactive inhibition." This effect can be counteracted, though, by making the newest material more meaningful. For instance, the employee is told at the end of the day that the last procedure could prove deadly if he or she makes a mistake. That warning places an entirely new level of importance on the instruction.

With interference, there is an opposite effect called "retroactive inhibition," which is when the interfering activity occurs after the learning period. In the previous example, the *first* procedure learned is interfered by the following 29 procedures. When learning, it is usually best not to take on too many new procedures until the earlier one is mastered. That is, when learning to ski, make certain you are comfortable with that skill before learning to surf or snowboard. Each skill requires a different set of coordinated movements; so, you don't want to confuse the movements of skiing with that of surfing.

Motivated forgetting is yet another concept regarding forgetfulness. This involves the person's reason for remembering or forgetting. If an event was too painful, the memory may become suppressed. Sad or traumatic events can be too agonizing to relive. Sometimes this can be a good thing since traumatic memories cause stress, and as previously discussed, too much stress damages health and the mind's ability to retain info.

The main reason, as will be the focus of this chapter, involves a lack of cues or guides in retrieving stored data. We are only able to recall information to the extent that something triggers the memories. Without those triggers, or cues, the memory becomes relatively inaccessible, almost as if we have lost the address to the house. Without the address (cue), we cannot find the house (memory).

Techniques to Overcome Forgetfulness

As revealed in Chapter 10 on note taking, the most potent memory aid is paper, in the form of notes. Simply write the detailed "things to remember" and reference it regularly to ensure you are reminded of everything. In this modern age, replace a paper planner with an electronic one, but be sure to have a backup in case the hard drive or memory card fails.

Imagination and humor can also keep important info in place. Suppose that this coming Thursday you have an appointment with a client, Mr. Patel. If you enjoy watching television in the evenings, imagine Mr. Patel acting like a clown, coming out of the TV screen saying, "See you on Thursday!" Or imagine Mr. Patel replacing a favorite character on a Wednesday night program. To add more staying power, imagine Mr. Patel on TV crossing the desert, thirsty (which sounds like "Thursday") for water. In this way, when you sit down in front of the tube on Wednesday evening, your mind will start replaying these images, thus reminding you of the appointment for the following day.

Associating an item with a routine is another way to prevent forgetting. For example, if you frequently forget to bring your cell phone to work, make it a point to put the cell phone inside your bag or briefcase each morning before brushing your teeth. Each time you go to brush, you will be reminded to put the phone in the bag.

To reinforce this activity, take your cell phone into the bathroom, pull out your toothbrush and toothpaste, and place everything on the counter side by side. Look at these three items and say, "Before brushing my teeth, put the cell phone in my bag." Then, pick up the cell phone and place it in the bag or briefcase.

Anytime you see the toothbrush or toothpaste, you'll think of the image of the cell phone next to these items on the counter, which will act as the cue to not forget it. Going through this motion will lodge the reminder securely into long-term unconscious storage.

Finally, go back into the bathroom, look at the toothbrush and ask, "Did I place my cell phone in my bag?" This will trigger the "warning" every time the toothbrush is seen. Repeat this procedure several times to make it stick.

Creating a hint is yet another way to help prevent forgetfulness. Suppose a guest is coming to dinner tomorrow night and you must stop at the grocery store after work to pick up potatoes for the dish you are preparing. The problem is, you have a habit of going on autopilot when leaving work, and as a result, often forget about running such errands and instead drive straight home.

In these instances, use hints to overcome such forgetfulness. Place a bag of potato chips or a toy potato on top of the television or in the middle of the dining room table to trigger the memory. Or put a small bag of potato chips in your briefcase as a hint. Better yet, place a toy potato on the dashboard of the car, as long as it does not become a distraction to driving. A visual with such specific placement can help elicit the after-work errand.

To further stave off forgetfulness, verbalize the task in your head or out loud. Perhaps you are extremely busy, with multiple deadlines looming, and need to ask a coworker a question when he returns from lunch. With all the priorities, though, you are afraid of forgetting to ask the coworker that important question.

The solution here is to repeat the task in your head or out loud: "Remember to stop by John's desk about the invoices." As you attend to other priorities, regularly verbalize the need to speak to John. Once all priorities have been addressed, the reminder will be in mind.

If you are nervous about forgetting, a tried and true method is to relax. Sometimes, forcing recall only makes it worse. If the realization that force only worsens the problem, because that is all you can think about, then try the reverse—imagine using all the force in the universe to push the memory away.

Imagine shoving that memory in a large, lockable safe at the other side of the universe and losing the key on the way back to this galaxy. The ridiculousness of the image can sometimes help one relax long enough to let the reminder come up. In addition to relaxing, this technique also helps one regain control over their focus.

One more solution is to get a companion. Those who have a solitary lifestyle can easily become absentminded. Without someone to talk to, one's mental activity is greatly reduced and not fully utilized. A pet can help, but an intelligent human companion can prove far more intellectually stimulating.

Discussing various topics, sharing knowledge and experiences, and taking part in similar activities can sharpen memory and enhance reminder skills. The companion can also act as a failsafe. "Remind me later that we have that party to go to," you might say. (And, of course, always be nice to your companion).

Overcoming Forgetfulness During Exams

Students already know how easily answers can elude them. Even with the use of memory aids, it is not uncommon to draw a blank on test day. This section seeks to change all that.

First, visualize success. Picture the exam complete and feeling really good about the outcome—a perfect score. See all of the information as if it were spread out on the table or desk before you. Imagine that each answer is easily accessible and can be read with no trouble, with all of the responses coming to you effortlessly.

The next step is to relax. If you find yourself worried, unable to remember anything, simply let go. Think of a place that exudes serenity and peace—snow in the mountains, a summer meadow, or a tranquil day at the beach. Before tackling a task requiring lots of memory access, like a college entrance exam, find a relaxation picture to help you find focus.

If relaxation does not seem even remotely possible, then try the reversal technique mentioned earlier. Jump into the fear by imagining the building collapsing on top of you or a plane crashing just outside—any massive distraction that greatly exaggerates the fear condition you're experiencing. The object is to put yourself in control of the feelings by creating the fear rather than suffering it. By being in control—at cause—you are no longer at the mercy of that fear. After regaining control, return to the relaxation technique.

To borrow a technique from the chapter on retrieval, practice the easy stuff. This will "prime the pump," so to speak, and get the information flowing again. Simply practice remembering anything— anything at all that comes to mind. Evoke what you had for breakfast, the last time you kissed your significant other, or better, the first time you kissed him or her. Then focus on the easy exam questions, or at least the ones that can be answered with little effort. Summoning any single fact greases the neural tracks for better retrieval.

The last tip is to borrow the exercise from the visualization chapter by closing your eyes and picturing yourself back in the location where you learned, heard, or came across the material, whether in class or the study hall, library, or café where you were studying.

CHAPTER THIRTEEN - REMEMBERING NAMES AND FACES

I joked about every prominent man of my time, but I never met a man I didn't like—Will Rogers

There is no doubt that we like to hear people call our name. There is something about feeling important enough to be thought of and remembered. On the other hand, it can feel hurtful when someone doesn't remember or refer to us by name. How would you feel if a friend or acquaintance called you by the wrong name?

This proves challenging for people in business or for those who depend upon others they meet. Meetings, business gatherings, and social events create opportunities to make connections, but those connections can be soured if they are not remembered. Not to mention, it can be embarrassing when others know your name, but you forget theirs. It can be even more embarrassing if you have to ask a person for his or her name, especially when you are clearly expected to know it already.

The same goes for faces. Imagine attending a seminar and meeting several very successful entrepreneurs. These are the leaders and the shakers of industry, but suddenly you cannot summon what they looked like. Embarrassing, right? When remembering people, therefore, it is important to recall not only names, but faces as well. This chapter presents techniques for both.

Remembering Names

To commit a person's name, apply all you've learned up to this point. First, start with attention. When a person says their name, realize that this moment is invaluable and will soon be gone, so pay attention as the name is spoken. Look at the person's lips as the name is being pronounced. For instance, if introduced to a man named Edgar Templeton, watch his lips pucker, squeeze, and tighten as he pronounces ED-gahr TEM-puhl-tun.

If you miss hearing the name, ask the person to repeat it. For some reason, people find it embarrassing to simply say, "I'm sorry, I didn't hear your name." There's nothing to be embarrassed about. Since a person's name is one of their most prized possessions, it's flattering to make even the slightest fuss over it. If nothing else, it shows that you're interested in them enough to get their name right.

Next, apply the repetition technique of remembering information on the fly. Begin by repeating the name back to the new acquaintance. If someone introducing himself says, "Hello, I'm Bill Anderson," respond with, "Nice to meet you, Mr. Anderson. May I call you Bill?" Notice how this response includes both the first and last name in a pleasant and natural way. This would be your first repetition.

Then, say the name in your thoughts. After, add the person's name to the conversation. Find an opportunity to respond to something your new acquaintance says: "That's interesting, Bill. I'd like to learn more." This nails the third repetition.

As the conversation continues, it might help to think of something to comment on or ask about the name of your new acquaintance. For instance, "Are you in any way related to the late Sir John Templeton of the Templeton Foundation?" Or "I had a friend named George Templeton in college. Do you know him?" Finding additional opportunities to repeat the name like this is great, but only if it comes across natural. Don't overdo it with any one person, or you may get strange looks.

As the conversation draws to a close, consider saying, "Well, Bill Anderson, it has been a real pleasure to meet you. I hope we meet again." In these ways, you have repeated the name several times, not only mentally, but also out loud. It will allow you to remember the name long enough to take additional action. Without this series of repetition, you may forget the name instantly.

Depending on how long you'd like to remember the name, apply other methods. Retrieve the name after the encounter and few more times throughout the day. You might add additional repetition by telling a friend, relative, or associate the name of the new acquaintance. It can be as straightforward as, "I just met Edgar Templeton."

Also, write the name down, either in a phone, notebook, or even on a napkin, because the mere act of writing will aid memory. Though it's better to note in a phone or notebook so you can refer to it later.

Another option is to apply the technique of association. Connect the name "Edgar" with someone famous, like the American writer Edgar Allen Poe. Associating this new person to a well-known or famous person creates a link to something already known, which increases the chances of remembering the name. Picturing Edgar Allen Poe and Sir John Templeton together reinforces the association and this new acquaintance.

In addition to the technique of association, apply the technique of visualization. Visualize the spelling of the name in your mind. Play with exaggerating and making the image humorous. For instance, picture Edgar Templeton bench pressing weights in the shape of his name.

Another way to incorporate visualization is to link the name with a visual object. In this case, "Ed" could be short for "Theodore" and another short form of Theodore is "Ted" or "Teddy." So, picture a teddy bear for the first part of the name. Next, "gar" might equate to "Garfield," so picture the infamous cartoon cat of the same name. Finally, picture a one-ton weight sitting on a temple—"temple" plus "ton"—with Garfield and a teddy bear dancing arm-in-arm in front. Such humorous images heighten interest in the elements used to secure the name.

All these instructions can seem like a lot, but realize each action of repeating, retrieving, noting, associating, and visualizing take only a few seconds to do. It's not the length of time that will be the challenge, just the matter of getting yourself to do it enough to develop the habit.

Remembering Faces

Now that you know how to remember someone's name, let's move on to the task of remembering that person's face. When a person states his or her name, after focusing on the pronunciation, immediately turn attention to the person's face. This quickly connects the name with the face, which helps associate a sound to something visual.

To go further, study the face for a moment and find something unique or interesting about it. Is it circular or square? Do they have dimpled cheeks? Are the eyebrows bushy or slender? Is the nose long or squat? Are the eyes small and beady or large and round, and are they set narrowly together or widely apart? Does the person's face remind you of anyone, or is it entirely unique? Consider also the shape and size of his or her physique. Is it heavyset, athletic, or petite?

Later in the day, well after the introduction, apply the technique of retrieval to visualize the faces of the people you met that day. Remember the details you paid attention to—the size and shape of their noses, the shape of their head, the size and spacing of their eyes, and more. Recall the setting and the ambiance in which you met the person. Such feelings can trigger memories of the person's appearance and other features. Practice this not only with people you meet, but also with strangers you casually encounter perhaps at a fast-food restaurant or the bank.

It helps to practice with photographs in newspapers and magazines. Cut out pictures of people with their names in the caption. Create a stack of two or three dozen pictures, then look at each one using the techniques discussed here to remember the faces and associated names. Then, like flash cards, look at the faces and attempt to recall their respective names, verifying the answer by looking at the caption included with the picture.

Interest

All too often, failing to remember people stems from a lack of interest. You may be fascinated with what they have to say and may even be enthralled with their importance, however, you simply do not find them interesting as a person. It's good to be interested in and to like people simply as people.

Hubert Humphrey, the consummate politician, almost became president of the United States, though he did reach the number two spot of vice president. He was also a United States senator for more than two decades and enjoyed a two-term stint as a popular mayor in Minneapolis.

The University of Minnesota alumni association described their "favorite son" in the following manner: "He was known for his almost supernatural ability to remember the homeliest face, commonest name, and most ordinary life story years after a first encounter."

One collector of Humphrey memorabilia noted, "When you meet people who met him over the years, they all tell the same story." Someone would have an encounter with the politician and discuss insignificant details about their life, like a cabin at the lake or what their children did for hobbies. "Then they'd see him a year later and he'd ask how the fishing was at ... and he'd name the lake—or ask how 'that Jerry of yours' is doing these days."

It blew people away. They were impressed by Humphrey's seemingly perfect memory and his uncanny ability to recognize constituents years after their first meeting.

How can you have a memory like Humphrey? As stated, it starts with interest. Learn to like people—genuinely and deeply. Cultivate an active interest in those you meet. By cultivating interest, the rest becomes easy.

A great way to cultivate interest in a person whose name you want to remember is to imagine the person planning to hand over an outrageous sum of money. Pretend that this new contact will offer you $1,000,000 next week. You certainly want to remember the person to remind him or her of the pledge.

Although this does not equate to direct interest, it's still a powerful trick to juice up the mind's appeal in a new acquaintance. Later, you may not have to resort to such tricks, but when starting out, it's worth a try.

The ability to recall people's names and faces is an important life skill. The techniques mentioned here are simple, but have been proven to be extremely effective. Try them at the next social or business event and witness the power of instant recall first hand.

CHAPTER FOURTEEN - REMEMBERING NUMBERS

It's clearly a budget. It's got a lot of numbers in it—George W. Bush

Modern society is built on numbers. Whether or not you are numerically inclined, there is no escaping the phone numbers, pin codes, postal codes, passwords, and many other aspects of daily life that depend on numbers.

Unlike words, numbers prove more difficult to remember because numbers are not tangible, so they cannot easily be associated with something physical or concrete. The word "baseball" is easy to picture. Numbers are more abstract and intangible, so if someone says 9873, it's difficult to create a meaningful image, let alone connect it to something concrete.

Nonetheless, there are ways to make numbers memorable, which is what this chapter uncovers. It presents creative ways to store numbers to keep you from getting bogged down by all the digits in your life.

Sight, Sound, Clustering, and Repetition

Remember clusters and repetition? Here is a refresher. Repeating a number several times can imprint that information—for example, "4893, 4893, 4893." But rather than say "four-eight-nine-three" or "four thousand eight hundred ninety-three," cluster the number into smaller pieces—"48" and "93." The smaller clusters of "forty-eight" and "ninety-three" is significantly easier to remember.

Furthermore, add the power of sight to the repetition. In addition to writing down the number several times, visualize the shapes of those numerals made of wood, written on a billboard, or fashioned into jewelry. Or imagine the numbers as the name of a television show.

To reinforce the number further, create a rhyme—"forty-eight, ninety-three, and make like a tree." Combine the rhyme with a visual of the numerals made out of branches of a tree or logs as shown:

"Forty-eight, ninety-three, and make like a tree."

The Art of Numerical Association

If the number has a built-in relationship to something you already know, then by all means, use it. For instance, if your mother's new address is 6626 Elm Street. In physics class, you happen to notice that the Planck constant is listed as 6.626 times 10 to the -34 power. Look familiar?

For those who happen to live in Lederach, Pennsylvania, the zip code is easy as long as residents know the year World War II ended—1945. Add a zero to the end to get—19450. Not everyone will be able to take advantage of such coincidences, but if they exist, why not take advantage?

Grouping System

The Grouping System combines clustering and associations, which is great for remembering numbers longer in length. With the system, break long numbers into smaller clusters, then associate each cluster with something familiar.

To memorize 299792458, the speed light travels in meters per second, first divide the number into smaller chunks, for instance: 299-7924-58. Next, connect each chunk to something recognizable.

For instance, 299 can be linked to $299, the price of your new desk. If interested in astronomy, as you most likely would to study the speed of light, associate 7924 with HD 7924, the extra solar planet discovered in the constellation of Cassiopeia. The number 58 could represent the jersey number of a favorite athlete, like Jack Lambert, the four-time Super Bowl champion of the Pittsburg Steelers.

Then to recall the number, simply connect the three different associations—price of your new desk, HD 7924, and Jack Lambert—to arrive at 299792458.

To illustrate with another example, let's take the first sixteen digits of Euler's consonant, 2.718281828459045. To use the Grouping System, consider clustering the number as follows: 2.7–1828–1828–45–90–45, and then make the following associations:

2.7—the standard approximation of e

1828—a leap year or the year when President Andrew Jackson won the election

1828—repeat of the year

45-90-45—a square cut diagonally in half produces a triangle with these angles

As you can see, the technique is simple. Cluster a lengthy series of digits into smaller, more manageable parts, and then associate each of the smaller parts to something familiar.

Converting Numbers to Words

One potent method for conserving numbers uses our old friend the acrostic. Do you recall "**M**y **V**ery **E**ducated **M**other **J**ust **S**erved **U**s **N**uts," the acrostic used to remember the sequence of the eight planets in the Solar system? By converting numbers into letters, you can create a sentence to remember those numbers. To apply the technique, first, pair individual numerals to letters of the alphabet like so:

A=1, B=2, C=3, D=4, E=5, F=6, G=7, H=8, I=9, J=0, K=1, L=2, M=3, N=4, O=5, P=6, Q=7, R=8, S=9, T=0, U=1, V=2, W=3, X=4, Y=5, Z=6.

To remember which letter pairs with which number, understand that it all starts with A=1, J=10 and T=20, though disregard the tens digit so that J=0 and T=0.

Next, take a number you want to remember and convert each of its digits to a corresponding letter. For each letter, come up with a word that, when put together, forms a sentence.

Let's observe the technique in action with the previous example of 4893. Convert 4 to (D, N or X), 8 to (H or R), 9 to (I or S), and 3 to (C, M or W). The acrostic you create is entirely up to you, but as usual, the more odd or humorous, the better. For this example, you might pick the letters N, H, I, and M to form the crazy sentence, "**N**o **H**uman **I**s **M**artian," which remains true until we colonize the red planet.

Granted, this technique requires a bit more work and practice, but such a technique allows one to easily store all types of numbers with great accuracy. When practicing, start with simple numbers to build familiarity before moving on to more complex ones.

Using a Picture Code

The next method associates an image to each numeral from zero to nine. Instead of associating a letter to a number, you are connecting it to an image that resembles the number in some way. For instance, the head and neck of a swan somewhat resembles the number 2, so a swan could make for a great association. The following table provides images for the other numbers. Notice how the shape of each numeral looks like the associated image.

ball = 0	magic wand = 1	swan = 2
fork = 3	sailboat = 4	seahorse = 5
bomb = 6	crowbar = 7	hourglass = 8

	balloon = 9 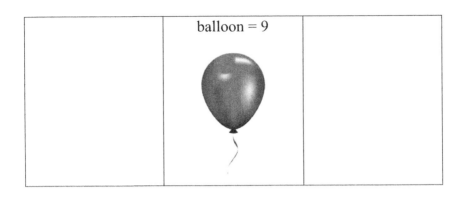	

To review an example using this method, suppose your new bank account PIN is 2495. First, picture a swan (2) towing a toy sailboat (4) tied to a large, red balloon (9), and dangling from the balloon is a rather bewildered seahorse (5). This series of images includes the exact numbers and sequence in the account PIN.

The Picture Code has the added burden of memorizing the list of associated pictures, though for visual learners, associating numbers to pictures is far easier than to letters, allowing them to remember all kinds of numbers and their sequence.

The Major Memory System

Like the method described in the subsection on "Converting Numbers to Words," the Major Memory System works by memorizing words and phrases instead of the numbers themselves. Unlike the other method, this one is not an exact number-to-letter connection, but rather a number-to-sound connection (phonetic). Each number from zero to ten is assigned a consonant. Then words or phrases are formed by replacing numbers with a constant and then adding a vowel between them.

The following list assigns a consonant sound to each number.

0 = s, z, soft-c ("z" is first letter of zero)

1 = t, th ("t" is similar to a 1 with a line through it)

2 = n ("n" has two bars)

3 = m ("m" has three bars)

4 = r ("r" is last letter of four)

5 = L ("L" is Roman numeral for 50)

6 = j, sh, ch, soft-g ("g" in some typefaces is 6 rotated 180 degrees)

7 = k ("k" looks like two 7s rotated and pasted together)

8 = f, v ("f" written in cursive has two loops similar to 8)

9 = p, b ("p" and "b" looks like 9 in different angles)

For each number, substitute the consonant associated to it. Next, add vowels in between to create a familiar word or phrase that makes sense and thus can be easily remembered.

For example, to remember the date the Gettysburg Address was delivered (11-19-1863), the number 1 can be substituted with "t" or "th." For the first 1 of 11, you might substitute "th," and for the next 1 sub in "t." Then add the vowel "a" in between to form the word "that."

With 19, the letters we have to work with are "t" & "th" for 1 and "p" & "b" for 9. You might use the letters "t" & "p" and add the vowel "o" in between to form the word "top."

With the year 1863, the number 1 can be substituted with "t" again, 8 with v, 6 with "g," and 3 with "m," to give the letters "t," "v," "g," and "m" to form the phrase "tv gem."

To remember the date, elicit the phrase "That Top TV Gem" to get 11-19-1863. Such a system is also useful for phone numbers or zip codes. Just create word sequences that are relevant to the numbers being remembered.

This sums up the discussion on memorizing numbers. Some of the suggestions offered here, like the Major Memory System, are somewhat complicated and involved, requiring practice to grasp. With enough repetition and practice, any of the systems can become natural and almost automatic to use. By seeing a phrase like "No Human Is Martian" or "That Top TV Gem," the mind will instantly make the conversion to 4893 and 11-19-1863 with little to no conscious effort. Though it takes work and dedication upfront to reach that level.

Also, keep in mind that any system is likely something that you will use for a lifetime. That means investing a little time in the right system now can provide a large return over the long haul.

CHAPTER FIFTEEN - REMEMBERING PLACES

There are places I remember all my life, though some have changed—The Beatles, *Rubber Soul* album

Some people seem gifted when it comes to remembering directions or finding their way back to a place they've visited only once. No matter how puzzling a path, they have no problem honing in on where they are and where they need to go.

The rest of us, however, are not so skilled. We experience trouble remembering our way even after several passes. If you experience such difficulties, you're in luck because this chapter offers methods for enhancing memory of routes, directions, and addresses.

Routes

What destroys most people's sense of a route is that they travel along rather absentmindedly, ignoring recognizable features and landmarks. This is particularly true if someone else is driving or if the person is on a route for the first time.

To better remember a route, take note of unique or familiar features you pass. Notice not only the directions of the streets, but also get a feel for how those directions relate to landmarks—both natural and manmade. Observe the distinctive hills or mountains in sight and whether there are familiar restaurants or maybe a favorite store along the way.

These features become associative cues that point to where you are. A favorite store will remind you that a turn is approaching or that you went too far and missed a turn. These cues can also be used to find your way back.

When traveling through a static terrain like a monotonous suburb, taking note of landmarks can be difficult, but not impossible. Even suburbs feature noteworthy differences like unique color schemes or house styles. Some homes might be split-level, some ranch style, while some two or three levels. Observe these variations, especially at intersections.

Also notice the style and size of street signs. Some signs are large, like those for busy major thoroughfares, while other signs can be quite small. Some signs are written in black letters on a white background, while many sport white letters on a green background. Notice these variations particularly at intersections.

A way to condition the mind for this kind of observation is to practice when walking or jogging around the neighborhood. When out, observe as much detail as possible, then after returning home, review the trip and recount everything you observed. You might even write down the details, or better still, draw a map of the route and label everything you remember, including the names of streets; size, shape, and colors of buildings; as well as other noteworthy features.

The next time you head out, take the map and compare what you drew to what is actually there. You will find that you are able to notice aspects of routes that went unnoticed before, and thus enhance recollection of those routes through which you travel.

Directions

The previous suggestions are great for remembering routes on which you've already traveled, but what if you are relying solely on directions someone has given, either verbally or in writing. In this case, the previous tips will not work as the route hasn't been taken and so landmarks have not been observed to use as hints.

Nonetheless, you can ask the person providing the directions to furnish such hints. If given the direction "to go down Rodeo Drive for five blocks and then turn left," ask for a landmark. Knowing there is a shopping mall on the left just before the turn, will make remembering that turn far easier. Also, the shopping mall will act as a cue because seeing the mall will indicate that a turn is ahead.

Now, directions don't just have one turn, they usually come in a string of unfamiliar left and rights. Recalling such a list of left and right turns amidst all the roads and intersections can be even more cumbersome. In addition to remembering where to turn, a driver must also remember whether to make a left or right.

So, it helps to translate the lefts and rights into memorable images. Translate lefts into something like "lions" and rights into "rabbits." At intersections that require making a left turn, picture a lion standing at the corner, and at intersections that require a right, picture a rabbit. This reinforces the direction to turn at each junction.

To take the suggestion one step further, for the number of blocks needed to travel before making the turn, picture that many lions or rabbits. When told to go down Rodeo Drive for five blocks and turn left after the shopping mall, picture five large lions standing outside the mall—five for the five blocks and "lions" for turning "left." If the next part of the directions entails driving three blocks before making a right at the gas station, picture three rabbits at the gas station.

To really make the route stick, exaggerate the images. Picture the lions in cowboy hats and boots and the rabbits in suits and ties. Images like these, however silly, make each turn distinct, and in turn, memorable. If you don't like "lions" and "rabbits," feel free to pick other animals or objects. The more personal, the better. Just make sure the words start with the same letters: "R" (for right) and "L" (for left). As always, practice is essential.

If the route contains numerous rights and lefts, weave them into a story. It helps to employ one of the number techniques, like the picture code, presented in the last chapter. Suppose a colleague gives the following directions for a fabulous new restaurant:

1. Drive 5 blocks down Rodeo Drive and hang a left at the mall.

2. Then, go down 9 blocks before making a right at the barber shop.

3. Finally, continue for 4 blocks until you see the restaurant on the right.

The story might go something like: A seahorse (5) is chasing a lion (left) at the mall. A balloon (9) is stuck to the tail of a rabbit (right) at a barber shop. There is now a boat (4) sailing by that very rabbit (right) just outside the restaurant.

Addresses

Employing the techniques in the last chapter, with a dash of personal creativity, can make remembering addresses a breeze. Suppose you want to remember the address of a new friend, 93 Mountainview Avenue. Begin by converting 93 into "Pam" (9=p, 3=m, with a vowel in between). For the word "Mountainview," picture a telescope on top of a mountain. Now put the two together and imagine Pam looking through the telescope on the mountain top.

If the town or city has made things difficult by having Mountainview Street right next to the Mountainview Avenue, associate an image to each road. "Avenue" might take on an aviation theme, because the words both start with "av." For the word "street," consider "steer" because both "street" and "steer" begin with "stee." "Avenue," then, is symbolized by an aviator or airplane, while "street" is by a bull (steer). In this example, visualize Pam on the mountain wearing an aviator's cap as she looks through the telescope.

To illustrate an address on Mountainview *Street*, for instance 843, you might convert the number to the word "farm" (8=f, 4=r, 3=m). With this address, visualize that same telescope on the mountain top, but picture it in the middle of a farm with a steer walking around it.

Not only are these simple techniques effective at remembering directions and addresses, but they also can be a lot of fun. With practice and commitment, using the techniques can become a passing thought.

CHAPTER SIXTEEN - REMEMBERING EVENTS

Do not seek to have events happen as you want them to, but instead want them to happen as they do happen, and your life will go well—
Epictetus, Greek stoic philosopher

Can you recall what you ate for dinner last weekend or the conversation you had with your spouse yesterday? If these events seem a bit hazy, you are not alone. Most people suffer this kind of memory lapse. With so many priorities tugging at our attention, it is easy to forget events of the day.

A potent method for remembering such information is to do a daily review. That is, take a few moments in the evening to recap everything that transpired in the day. Such a recap is a form of retrieval. If you remember, retrieval is a powerful way to both engage the mind and stimulate formation of long-range memories. Recap of the day's event repeats the experiences, and thus, flags them as important, making even minor incidents impossible to forget.

To do this, each evening think about everything that happened earlier in the day. Spend 5–10 minutes calling to mind all the significant details that occurred. Perform the exercise when the day is winding down and no other pressing issues require immediate attention. It helps to be alone so distractions and interruptions don't get in the way.

Because there is a likelihood for the mind to drift on such a task, it helps to write down the daily events rather than merely reviewing them in mind. To that end, keep a notepad next to the coffee table, night stand, or where you are likely to do the exercise. After work or just before retiring for the night, grab that notepad and start jotting down the fine points.

So, what should you write? Everything from what you had for breakfast to the argument with your spouse to the people you met along the way. Record where you went for lunch, the conversation at the watercooler, and any notable events in between. If you received a parking ticket, note that. If you bought a pair of shoes you had been eyeing, note that as well.

The first time you attempt the exercise, such details may not come up. You may not even be able to recall what was on your dinner plate just a few hours earlier. In such situations, combine the techniques of visualization and retrieval by picturing yourself back at the office, class, dinner table, with friends, talking to family, or in the grocery store and notice all the memories that are triggered. As they arise, write them down.

Outside of affirmations, this is the most important activity for improving memory. If you spend 5–10 minutes each evening retrieving the events of the day, you will begin remembering more of what you see, hear, learn, do, and more of what transpires during the day. It will happen naturally.

That's because by developing a habit of reviewing the day's events, the mind realizes that it will be called upon for such specifics later in the evening, so it will be more conscious about what happens during the day and work to hold on to those experiences, instead of merely discarding 80% within a few hours. If you really want to supercharge your memory, do this exercise every evening.

To add additional staying power, perform the daily review again the next morning before getting out of bed. The added repetition will deepen the neural pathways to keep the memories going stronger and longer.

Though an even better alternative to performing a daily review twice a day is to perform the review once in the evening, before falling asleep, and in the morning, repeat the set of affirmations provided in

Chapter 3. If you can do these two things every day, day-in-and-day-out, you will have an incredible memory. You will remember most anything with immense detail and clarity.

In fact, memory improvement doesn't get easier than this! Notice the exclamation mark in the previous sentence. I rarely use exclamations in my writing. Only when I really want to stress something, and I can't stress these two combinations enough. Repeating affirmations and performing retrieval daily will give you the memory you sought when picking up this book. Best of all, both suggestions are very easy and simple, taking only 5 to 10 minutes out of your morning and evening.

In addition to thinking about or writing down the daily review, it helps to talk to someone about it. Talking to someone forces a person to more accurately recall their experiences, which in turn helps one remember them more accurately. If the other person is truly interested in your day, it will motivate you to remember even more. Though, be polite—don't talk only about yourself and what happened to you, but rather engage the other side and ask about their day as well.

CONCLUSION

A conclusion is the place where you get tired of thinking—Arthur Bloch, an American writer

Alas this book has come to an end. Certainly, you learned a wide range of techniques for improving memory. Now, for a technique to be practical, not only must it be simple to learn, it must be simple to apply. If a technique is neither, it will provide little value. In this modern era, we have too much on our plate to take excessive amounts of time and energy to learn difficult and time-consuming instructions. Memory techniques are no exception.

This is the reason I wrote the book. I believe there are an abundance of useful tools to improve memory, intelligence, and learning that can make people's lives easier and better. The goal was to present these tools in ways that readers could quickly grasp and easily apply with the type of information they regularly encounter. Only then will the techniques be beneficial.

The next step is to integrate the information. A good way to do that is by rereading this book several times. Realize that you've likely already forgotten at least 50% of the suggestions, if not more. With each day, you will lose even more. So, revisiting the material is essential in maintaining what you do remember and restoring what you've lost.

In this way, you don't have to put a whole lot of effort into remembering the ideas or in how to use them. The simple act of rereading the book will lock the techniques in mind. So, when faced with something noteworthy, the proper technique and its application will instantly appear.

In addition, rereading helps you catch important points that may have been missed. One can never grasp everything from a book in a single pass. The first time a book is read, the mind is focused primarily on making sense of the new information. It is unable to immerse itself in the details as it is working to understand the basics.

With each additional pass, the mind can go further. The repeated experience allows the brain to delve deeper into the content to truly comprehend what the author is trying to say. Rereading yields a far better understanding of the techniques—what to do, how they work, and where to apply them.

So how should you approach rereading? Start by reading this book a second time now. Then in a week, read it again. After a month, do it another time. Then read the book once more in three months.

This sequence will create enough repetitions to allow the suggestions to sink in, which will result in fewer struggles when applying them. The book is designed to be easy to read and digest, and is not terribly long, so going through it a few times should be fairly painless.

If you are sincere about improving and maintaining a strong, healthy memory, reread this book regularly after the initial three-month period. Don't make the mistake of using it like a novel that you read only once, but rather as a reference manual that you revisit often. Whenever you need a refresher or to hone your skills, come back to it.

I also recommend listening to the audio edition of this book. Hearing the audio is a powerful way to reinforce the material because it brings into play the power of the auditory sense. Studies show that we understand what we hear better than what we read. The audio will also make it easier to regularly review the material as you simply have to press play on the audio player.

In addition to listening, a good approach is to start with techniques that are easy and natural, or ones that you enjoy. Or start with ones from which you expect to derive the most benefit. This will get you comfortable applying the information.

Once you master a technique or set of techniques, move on to a different one. Keep practicing until each method becomes familiar. When these suggestions become second nature, you will begin to easily remember recipes, telephone numbers, people's names, and more.

Keep in mind that no one technique is "right" or "wrong." Each reader will find that one works better for them than others, while some work better in certain situations than others.

Furthermore, don't be afraid to adapt the suggestions to your own situation and preferences. There are so many memory tools out there that I could have written a book ten times this size. I opted instead to offer strong fundamentals on the topic while providing real world examples of their application. This way, each reader can take the information and apply it to his or her own situation. So, feel free to vary the techniques and combine them in ways that best fit you and your needs.

Lastly, just as with learning anything, unless you put the techniques into practice, they will not serve you. You could study a car manual and learn every detail about that car, but unless you actually get behind the wheel to practice driving, negotiating traffic will be difficult. So, make sure to practice the techniques and practice memorizing every day. Look around for material to memorize. It could be as simple as a friend's phone number, a favorite dessert recipe, spelling of a new word, or even bullet points for an upcoming presentation.

Work at it, yes, but don't forget to have fun with it too.

I sincerely hope you enjoyed this book and found the presentation worthwhile. If you did, it would be helpful if you could leave a positive review of this book on Amazon. It only takes a few minutes, and it only need be a few words, but your positive feedback is invaluable.

Additional Resources

If you haven't downloaded your bonus *Triple Your Reading, Memory, and Concentration in 30 Minutes* you can do so at MindLily.com/me. It's a free guide that compliments the information here to take your memory to new heights.

Also check out these other books to enhance learning, memory, and productivity:

Speed Reading: Learn to Read a 200+ Page Book in One Hour

Concentration: Maintain Laser Sharp Focus and Attention for Stretches of 5 Hours or More

Mind Maps: Quicker Notes, Better Memory, and Improve Learning 3.0

Mind Mapping: Improve Memory, Concentration, Communication, Organization, Creativity, and Time Management

Made in the USA
Monee, IL
10 December 2022

20761807R00085